Layman's Bible Book Commentary
Ezekiel, Daniel

LAYMAN'S BIBLE BOOK COMMENTARY

LBBC

EZEKIEL, DANIEL
VOLUME 12

F. B. Huey, Jr.

BROADMAN PRESS
Nashville, Tennessee

Dewey Decimal Classification: 224.4

Subject Headings: BIBLE. O. T. EZEKIEL//BIBLE. O. T. DANIEL

Library of Congress Catalog Card Number: 81-66848

Printed in the United States of America

Foreword

The *Layman's Bible Book Commentary* in twenty-four volumes was planned as a practical exposition of the whole Bible for lay readers and students. It is based on the conviction that the Bible speaks to every generation of believers but needs occasional reinterpretation in the light of changing language and modern experience. Following the guidance of God's Spirit, the believer finds in it the authoritative word for faith and life.

To meet the needs of lay readers, the *Commentary* is written in a popular style, and each Bible book is clearly outlined to reveal its major emphases. Although the writers are competent scholars and reverent interpreters, they have avoided critical problems and the use of original languages except where they were essential for explaining the text. They recognize the variety of literary forms in the Bible, but they have not followed documentary trails or become preoccupied with literary concerns. Their primary purpose was to show what each Bible book meant for its time and what it says to our own generation.

The Revised Standard Version of the Bible is the basic text of the *Commentary,* but writers were free to use other translations to clarify an occasional passage or sharpen its effect. To provide as much interpretation as possible in such concise books, the Bible text was not printed along with the comment.

Of the twenty-four volumes of the *Commentary,* fourteen deal with Old Testament books and ten with those in the New Testament. The volumes range in pages from 140 to 168. Four major books in the Old Testament and five in the New are treated in one volume each. Others appear in various combinations. Although the allotted space varies, each Bible book is treated as a whole to reveal its basic message with some passages getting special attention. Whatever plan of Bible study the reader may follow, this *Commentary* will be a valuable companion.

Despite the best-seller reputation of the Bible, the average survey of Bible knowledge reveals a good deal of ignorance about it and its primary meaning. Many adult church members seem to think that its study is intended for children and preachers. But some of the newer translations have been making the Bible more readable for all ages. Bible study has branched out from Sunday into other days of the week, and into neighborhoods rather than just in churches. This *Commentary* wants to meet the growing need for insight into all that the Bible has to say about God and his world and about Christ and his fellowship.

BROADMAN PRESS

Contents

EZEKIEL

DANIEL

Introduction

EZEKIEL

Introduction

Of all the Old Testament prophets, none seems more strange or more difficult to understand than the prophet Ezekiel. Some scholars describe him as a visionary and mystic. His frequent visions set him apart from the experiences of most of us. He was a man of rigid self-discipline and obedience to God's orders. Nothing God requested seemed too difficult for him to do. From the first moment of his call, he was gripped by a passionate zeal for God. For example, he did not hesitate to make a public spectacle of himself by shaving off his hair (5:1-4) because God told him to do it. Another time, he controlled his tears at his wife's death in order to demonstrate to the people God's attitude toward Jerusalem's fall (24:16).

If such behavior at times seems unusual, it should remind us that a person totally committed to God will always run the risk of being labeled "strange."

Ezekiel's messages are often difficult to understand. Even ancient Jewish scholars had difficulties with them. Hananiah ben Hezekiah burned no less than three hundred jars of "midnight" oil poring over the book night after night. He was trying to resolve all the difficulties he found in it.

The rabbis forbade anyone under thirty years of age to read the beginning and end of the book. They did not believe that a person less mature could understand the visions that are found in those chapters!

Understanding the Prophets

There is much misunderstanding about the prophets of Israel. Some people think they were almost supernatural beings. They believe the prophets were concerned only about predicting with incredible accuracy events that would happen centuries later. At the other extreme are those who insist that there was nothing special about Israel's prophets. They were only the "preachers" and fortune-tellers of their times, nothing more.

The fact is that the prophets were both unique and human. They could be extremely courageous in the face of death (Jer. 38:6). They could also run and hide in fear for their lives (1 Kings 19:1-3).

The prophets were spiritually tuned to hear God speak to them. They were faithful in communicating "Thus says the Lord" to their people. They were the "preachers" of their times—teaching, exhorting, warning, and interceding. They did not hesitate to accuse the people of their sins of exploitation, immorality, and idolatry. They were also foretellers. They had spiritual insight to speak about things that were about to happen (Isa. 7:1-8). They could also speak about things that were going to happen in the distant future (Mic. 5:2; Zech. 14:4).

The prophets exercised their ministries with the confidence that God had chosen them and called them (Jer. 1:5). They sometimes questioned God about the afflictions they endured, but none of them ever questioned his call. In fact, it was the conviction that God had chosen him that often kept a prophet from giving up. Each of the prophets was gripped with a desire to please God, not people, at any cost. The prophets' singleness of devotion caused them to be misunderstood, ridiculed, and abused. Sometimes they were put to death by their own people (Luke 13:34).

Ezekiel was one of the prophets.

Ezekiel the Man

Very little is known about the personal life of Ezekiel. Nothing is known about his family except that his father was named Buzi (1:3). Ezekiel was a priest called to be a prophet while in exile in Babylon. His name means "God strengthens." He was carried into captivity to Babylon in 597 BC. There he spent the next five years pondering the calamity that had overtaken his people. Then one day while he was sitting on the banks of the river Chebar, God appeared to him in the midst of a storm cloud. He saw God seated on a throne and heard God speak to him. He was perhaps thirty years of age when the Lord appeared and called him to be a prophet (1:1).

For more than twenty years Ezekiel continued to be the Lord's spokesman in faraway Babylon. He was married, but his wife died suddenly about the time of the fall of Jerusalem in 587 BC. If he had children, they are not mentioned. He lived a simple life in his own house in Babylon. After his warnings about Jerusalem's destruction had come to pass, he enjoyed a brief time of popularity with his people (33:30-33).

Ezekiel was a contemporary of Jeremiah and Daniel. Nothing is known about the date or circumstances of Ezekiel's death. There is a Jewish tradition that he was put to death by his own people because of his preaching.

Ezekiel and His Times

In order to understand the Book of Ezekiel, it is important to know something about the times in which he lived.

The closing years of the seventh century BC were a time of crisis and turmoil in the ancient Near East. Assyria had dominated the known world for over 125 years. However, in 612 BC this dreaded superpower was conquered by her neighbor to the south, the Babylonians. Egypt challenged Babylon's supremacy, but at the battle of Carchemish in 605 BC Egypt was decisively beaten. For the next 65 years Babylon was the unchallenged major world power.

Against this background of international turmoil and intrigue, little Judah fought for survival. Her kings maintained a semblance of independence by paying tribute to Babylon. However, in 598 BC, after King Jehoiakim refused to continue paying tribute, Nebuchadnezzar sent an army against Jerusalem to put down the rebellion. Jehoiakim died, and his son, Jehoiachin, surrendered in order to spare the city. Jehoiachin and other leaders were taken as hostages to Babylon. Among them was Ezekiel, who, so far as is known, never returned to Jerusalem.

Ten years passed, but despite warnings by Ezekiel and Jeremiah, Judah continued to disobey the Lord. As punishment for her disobedience, Jerusalem, along with the sacred Temple, was destroyed by the Babylonians in 587 BC. Judah ceased to exist as an independent nation and became a province of the Babylonian empire. Many of the people were carried away as exiles. Some fled to Egypt, and others remained in Judah, where they struggled for survival in the devastated land. The next fifty years under Babylonian domination were difficult times for the people of God. The Jews in Babylon, however, enjoyed a better life than their kinsmen who remained in Judah. As evidence of their good treatment, when the

Persian successors to the Babylonians allowed the exiles to return to their own country in 538 BC, many preferred to remain where they were.

Ezekiel the Author

The ministry of Ezekiel is divided into two periods. Each period affected the emphasis of his messages. From the time of his call in 593 BC to the fall of Jerusalem in 587 BC marks one period. During those years his messages emphasized a warning of God's coming judgment on Judah.

With the destruction of Jerusalem, the prophet's ministry entered a second phase. The people had been devastated by defeat and loss of national identity. They did not need further reminders of the calamity they had brought on themselves. Instead, they needed some comforting words. Ezekiel's emphasis changed from judgment to future hope for Israel. He spoke of a restored nation and a restored Temple in the closing chapters. The second phase of his ministry continued at least until 571 BC. His last dated message was recorded in that year (see 29:17).

Ezekiel was an organized, orderly person. His messages are for the most part carefully dated and arranged in sequence. His book is composed of four clearly distinguishable divisions. The first contains prophecies of judgment on Judah and Jerusalem (chs. 1—24). These messages were delivered before the fall of Jerusalem. The second division is a collection of messages of judgment against seven foreign nations (chs. 25—32).

The third division begins after the fall of Jerusalem. It contains Ezekiel's words of encouragement to the people about Israel's restoration (chs. 33—39). The fourth and final division brings the book to a close on a triumphant note in Ezekiel's vision of a new Temple and a restored Israel (chs. 40—48).

Ezekiel liked to use certain phrases repeatedly. "They [you] will know that I am the Lord" is found more than sixty times. "I the Lord have spoken, and I will do it" occurs over forty times. "The Word of the Lord came to me" is also used over forty times. "As I live, says the Lord" occurs about fifteen times. Ezekiel preferred to speak in simple, plain prose. Isaiah and other prophets frequently used the more majestic poetic form to communicate their messages.

Attempts by some scholars to deny Ezekiel as author of the book that bears his name have been unsuccessful. The inner consistency and the uniformity of style and language throughout the book affirm its unity and authenticity.

The Influence of Ezekiel

Ezekiel apparently was respected by many in the exilic community in Babylon. He did not experience the kind of hostility and threats that Jeremiah did. At least, if he did, he did not mention them. The elders consulted him (8:1; 14:1; 20:1). The people flocked to hear him after his prophecies concerning Jerusalem's fall had come true (33:30-33).

Whatever his influence was in his lifetime, there is no question that Ezekiel exerted a profound influence on later Judaism. His insistence that God's people should be separate became a fixed conviction of the Jewish people. His emphasis on the elevation of religious over civil authority also prevailed. Some efforts have been made to link him with the origin of the synagogue, but without success. Some scholars say that Ezekiel rather than Ezra deserves to be called "the father of Judaism."

Except for the Book of Revelation (for example, 20:8; 22:1-2), Ezekiel's influence on the New Testament is not too apparent. Jesus' use of the Good Shepherd to describe himself has been linked to Ezekiel 34. Our Lord's use of the title "Son of man" for himself may have been influenced by Ezekiel, although many believe its origin is found in Daniel or a nonbiblical source called the Book of Enoch.

Messages of Judgment on Judah and Jerusalem
1:1 to 24:27

Ezekiel's Call and Commission (1:1 to 3:27)

The best way to understand what motivated a prophet is to examine his call. All the calls of the prophets in the Old Testament are not described, but those that are should be carefully studied (for example, Moses, Ex. 3:1 to 4:17; Samuel, 1 Sam. 3; Isaiah, Isa. 6;

Jeremiah, Jer. 1; and Ezekiel, Ezek. 1:1 to 3:15).

A careful study will show that no two call experiences were exactly alike, but that some characteristics were common to all of them. One of these was that God always took the initiative in setting aside a man to the prophetic office. No true prophet deliberately set about to seize the prophetic mantle for himself. None seemed to be expecting a call, and some of them vigorously resisted their call (for example, Moses, Jonah, and Jeremiah). Another common characteristic was that God did not force any person to be a prophet against his will. Each one was free to accept or to reject the call. However, having accepted it, a man became keenly aware of the divine compulsion to remain with the task (Jer. 20:9).

Although he was God's spokesman, a prophet discovered that his messages were not always popular or favorably received. For instance, Amos was accused of preaching for pay (Amos 7:12). Jeremiah was called a liar by his own people (Jer. 43:2). The people came to Ezekiel to be entertained, not to hear the word of the Lord (Ezek. 33:32).

The call of Ezekiel is described in the first three chapters of his book. A careful study of this event helps to explain Ezekiel's unyielding obedience to God.

An Unexpected Encounter with God (1:1-28)

The time and place (1:1-3).—Ezekiel had been taken to Chaldea (another name for Babylon) along with King Jehoiachin and other Judeans in 597 BC. It was the fifth year of the Exile, 593 BC, when heaven opened and Ezekiel saw visions of God. He was sitting at the time on the banks of the river Chebar, an irrigation canal that provided water essential for the cultivation of the land. The "thirtieth year" (v. 1) may be the prophet's age, or it may be a date calculated from an earlier event known to Ezekiel.

The vision is introduced by an unusual statement—"the word of the Lord came"—to Ezekiel (v. 3). The phrase suggests that the vision was more than a visual experience for the young man. It was a living reality that encompassed him completely. A feeling of compulsion to do God's will gripped him that felt like a "hand of the Lord" pressing upon him.

Four living creatures (1:4-14).—As Ezekiel peered into a storm cloud from the north that was rapidly enveloping him, he saw strange creatures with human forms. These creatures are identified in chapter 10 as cherubim. Each one had four faces and four wings that enabled it to go straight forward in any direction without turning as it went. Each face was different. One was human; the others were the faces of a lion, a bull, and an eagle. The creatures went wherever the spirit went without turning. Fire and lightning seemed to be flashing in their midst, and they gleamed like polished metal.

A chariot and its wheels (1:15-21).—The living creatures accompanied a vehicle, which is usually identified as a chariot. Each gleaming wheel seemed to be within another at a right angle so that it could move in any direction without turning. The rims were full of eyes, suggesting God's all-seeing knowledge. When the living creatures moved, the wheels moved also. The description of the vision is difficult to visualize, for what is being described is without parallel in human experience.

God on a throne (1:22-28).—Over the chariot was a platform (the word is usually translated as "firmament"). It was as clear as gleaming crystal. Underneath it, the moving wings of the creatures sounded like a rushing torrent of water or the noise of an encamped army. Ezekiel then saw a throne on or above the platform. The throne resembled sapphire (in Hebrew lapis lazuli, a stone of a rich blue hue). On the throne was seated one whom Ezekiel took momentarily to be a man. However, from the fiery, radiant appearance of the one on the throne, Ezekiel realized that he was seeing God. The radiant glow around the throne was like the colors of a rainbow. Ezekiel was so overwhelmed by this glorious appearance of the living Lord that he fell on his face in awe. He heard a voice speaking to him and knew it was the Lord.

It is difficult to visualize some of the details of Ezekiel's vision because they do not conform to anything we have seen or experienced. However, the vision clearly communicates to us the splendor of God and his irresistible power that is at work in the world. It also tells us that God is not limited to any single geographical area, as was commonly believed about deities in the ancient world. He could appear to a young exile in faraway Babylon as well as to a worshiper in the Temple at Jerusalem.

Assignment of a Difficult Task (2:1 to 3:27)

God did not appear to Ezekiel to satisfy his idle curiosity or to give him a mystical experience he could talk about the rest of his life. God appeared to Ezekiel to commission him as his spokesman.

A rebellious and unresponsive people (2:1-7).—Ezekiel heard the
Lord call him "son of man." The Lord addressed Ezekiel by this title
about ninety times in the book. He never called the prophet by his
name. The phrase has usually been understood to refer to the frailty
or mortality of Ezekiel as a human being. It may also suggest that
Ezekiel was related to the human race (if "man" is understood as
"mankind") and, therefore, had a responsibility to warn his people of
coming judgment. Jesus' use of the term as a favorite name for
himself has usually been linked to Daniel 7:13. However, Jesus may
have intended to emphasize his relationship and responsibility to
the human race as "Son of man." He took upon himself the likeness
of men (Phil. 2:7) and related himself voluntarily with the human
race. He willingly assumed the redemptive responsibility given him
by his Father, "to seek and to save the lost" (Luke 19:10). It is,
therefore, possible that Jesus was remembering Ezekiel when he
applied the title "Son of man" to himself.

God did not want Ezekiel to remain prostrate before him and
ordered him to stand on his feet (compare Job 38:3), for God
preferred to speak face to face. As he stood, Ezekiel sensed the
Spirit entering his body, energizing him for the task.

Ezekiel's task was going to be difficult and discouraging. God
informed him that he was sending him to the rebellious Israelites, a
people who had a history of rebellion. Moreover, they were
stubborn and obstinate (v. 4; literally, "hard of face and strong of
heart").

Ezekiel was instructed to preface his words to Israel with "Thus
says the Lord God" (v. 4). Ancient rulers frequently introduced the
public reading of their decrees with an authoritative "Thus says the
king of . . ." (see 2 Kings 18:19). Those who heard the decree
understood their obligation to obey because it carried the authority
of the king. Prophets frequently began with "Thus says the Lord" to
remind their audiences of the source of their authority and of the
people's obligation to obey.

Ezekiel was given no guarantee that the people would listen to
him. However, the Lord assured him that they would know that a
prophet had been among them (v. 5). When judgment fell, they
would remember that they had been warned (see Amos 3:7).

The Lord prepared Ezekiel for their unresponsiveness and for their defiance. God compared them to thistles, thorns, and scorpions (v. 6). He insisted, however, that Ezekiel was not to fear them. Ezekiel's responsibility was to speak God's messages to rebellious Israel. He was not to be anxious about their unresponsiveness or their threatening attitude toward him.

A scroll to eat (2:8 to 3:3).—In addition to a positive command to hear what God said to him, Ezekiel was warned not to be rebellious like Israel. A prophet commissioned to call a rebellious people back to God could not himself be rebellious (Jer. 15:19). Moses, Jonah, and Jeremiah had all initially shown reluctance to obey God's call, but Ezekiel showed no hesitation to accept the prophetic mantle.

In an act symbolizing Ezekiel's total identification with God's word, the Lord instructed him to open his mouth and eat a scroll that was offered to him (v. 8; compare Rev. 10:8-10). Two of the most commonly used writing materials in the ancient world were clay tablets and scrolls. The latter were made of papyrus, leather, or other materials. A scroll was usually no more than thirty feet in length and about ten inches wide.

Ordinarily a scroll was written on one side only. This one had writing on the front and back (v. 10; compare the huge visionary scroll of Zech. 5:1-4 that was full of curses). The unusual feature of writing on both the front and the back of this scroll may have symbolized the extensiveness of the judgment that was in store for the rebellious people of Judah. It may have suggested that the person who was given such a scroll could add no words of his own to it. The meaning of the words written on the scroll was clear. They were words of lament, mourning, and woe that announced Judah's coming punishment.

When Ezekiel opened his mouth and ate the scroll, he discovered that it was sweet as honey to his taste. It is difficult to understand how messages of judgment and doom could be "sweet" to a prophet. It probably meant that the sweetness was found in doing God's will. Jeremiah also described his reception of God's word in similar terms (Jer. 15:16; see also Ps. 119:103). There is an inward satisfaction found in doing God's will, although the task itself may be unpleasant.

A stubborn people (3:4-11).—Having received God's words, Ezekiel was then ready to communicate them to the "house of Israel" (v. 4; "Israel" here means all the covenant people, rather than the Northern Kingdom, which had ceased to exist after 722 BC).

God reminded the prophet that his audience did not speak a different language which could not be understood. He assured Ezekiel that foreigners would listen to him more readily than his own people. The barrier of a foreign language would have been easier to overcome than the rebellious spirit of the people of Judah. The Lord knew they would not listen because of their hard heads and stubborn hearts (v. 7).

The prospects must have seemed dismal to Ezekiel, but the Lord promised that he would make Ezekiel just as hardheaded as the people. He would be as hard as "adamant," an unknown substance of great hardness (v. 9). The Lord always gives his servants the resources they need to do his work. Armed with his spiritual resources, Ezekiel would have the courage to stand against all persecution and ridicule his people might heap upon him. The important thing for Ezekiel was to listen carefully with an open heart to all that God would speak to him (v. 10).

Ezekiel's reaction to the vision (3:12-15).—The meeting between the Lord and Ezekiel was at an end. The glorious presence of the Lord departed as the Spirit lifted up Ezekiel. The sound of the wings of the departing living creatures and the rumbling chariot wheels was like a great earthquake. As the Spirit bore him away, he felt a "bitterness in the heat of my spirit" (v. 14). A similar expression is used elsewhere to describe the anger of a bear robbed of her cubs (2 Sam. 17:8). Here it has been interpreted to mean Ezekiel's anger at the message God had given him. However, it more likely means he experienced the same kind of anger that God felt toward the rebellious people of Judah.

The Spirit brought him to Tel-abib, where other exiles like himself lived. He was so overwhelmed by what he had experienced that he sat among the people for seven days without saying a word. He was trying to understand all that had happened to him.

The prophet as watchman (3:16-21).—At the end of the seven days, the Lord spoke to Ezekiel again. The nature of his appearance to Ezekiel is not described this time. There may have been no visible manifestation of God as there had been at the river Chebar.

The Lord informed Ezekiel that he had made him a watchman for the house of Israel (see comment on 3:4). Ezekiel understood that as "watchman" he was being summoned to warn his people of God's impending judgment. In the ancient world the watchman had a very responsible duty. He stood on the wall surrounding the city and looked carefully in all directions for signs of approaching danger. If he saw an enemy approaching, he sounded the alarm to warn the people inside the city. They would shut the city gate and prepare for defense. If the watchman went to sleep or in any way failed to warn the people of the danger, the city would be taken by surprise and the people killed or enslaved.

Like a watchman, Ezekiel understood that his responsibility was to deliver God's words of warning to the people. If Ezekiel failed to warn a wicked person of impending punishment, that one would die, but God would require his blood from Ezekiel (v. 18). The meaning of the warning to Ezekiel is not certain, but it is ominous. It does suggest that he would be held accountable for his failure to speak out. On the other hand, if the prophet gave warning, but the wicked person did not turn from his wickedness, he would, of course, die; but Ezekiel would not bear any responsibility for his death (v. 19).

If a righteous man turned away from his righteousness, the prophet would be held accountable if he failed to warn him (v. 20). If the righteous man heeded Ezekiel's warning not to sin, that man would live; and Ezekiel would not be punished (v. 21). "Righteousness" in the Old Testament is not identical with the imputed righteousness of the New Testament that cannot be taken from a believer. The Old Testament person was righteous who fulfilled his obligations under the covenant (see 18:5-9 for Ezekiel's description of a righteous person).

The speechless prophet (3:22-27).—The Lord instructed Ezekiel to go to a certain valley-plain where he could speak further with the newly commissioned prophet. The exact location of the meeting place is not identified. There God's glory appeared to Ezekiel as it had at the river Chebar. As before, Ezekiel reacted by falling prostrate on his face. The Lord's Spirit entered the prophet and stood him on his feet.

The Lord instructed Ezekiel to shut himself in his own house. He would be bound there like a prisoner and not go out among the people. In addition to his isolation, Ezekiel's ability to speak was taken away so that he could speak only when God permitted. Ezekiel's "dumbness" lasted for seven and one-half years until word came that Jerusalem had fallen (33:21-22). His isolation in his home did not mean that he would be cut off from all contact with his people. They came to him on numerous occasions for advice and to hear God's words (8:1; 14:1; 20:1).

Warnings of Coming Judgment (4:1 to 7:27)

The period of preparation for his ministry had ended. It was now time for Ezekiel to act. He must get the attention of a people whom God had already described as hardheaded and stubborn (3:7). If they would hear his warnings, Ezekiel felt confident that they would mend their ways and return to God. He thought that surely they would not risk God's judgment if they were warned.

Symbolic Announcements of Judah's Fate (4:1 to 5:17)

In order to get the people's attention, Ezekiel's first warning messages were communicated to them by means of symbolic acts. A symbolic act is an enactment in "miniature" to represent the actual deed that God is going to perform. Its meaning could not be missed even by the most casual observer. For example, when Saul accidentally tore the garment of the prophet Samuel, Samuel used the accident as a symbolic act to announce that the kingdom was being torn away from Saul (1 Sam. 15:27-28).

Ezekiel and Jeremiah used symbolic acts more than any of the other prophets to transmit God's' revelatory messages to their people. However, they, like all the other prophets, did not limit themselves to any single means of proclaiming God's messages. Oral proclamation was the most usual way of announcing a word from the Lord, usually introduced by "Thus says the Lord." Even a symbolic act was interpreted orally by the prophet to those who witnessed it to be sure they understood its meaning.

The siege of Jerusalem (4:1-3).—The Lord instructed Ezekiel to perform his first symbolic act. He told him to take a clay brick and draw a sketch of Jerusalem on it. There was nothing unusual about drawing pictures on clay bricks. Messages were commonly inscribed on clay bricks in the ancient Near East by means of a sharp instrument called a stylus. This was done while the clay was still soft.

Ezekiel was then instructed to depict Jerusalem as though it were under siege by an enemy. He may have made miniature replicas of siegeworks, enemy camps, and battering rams and placed them around the brick. It is more likely that he drew a picture on the clay brick of a city under siege.

Then the Lord instructed Ezekiel to take an iron plate, such as was commonly used for baking bread, and to place it between himself and the brick that represented Jerusalem under siege. The clay tablet and the iron plate would serve as a sign to the people. God was warning them that Jerusalem was going to be besieged and taken by an invading army. They would cry out to God during that terrible crisis, but he would not hear them. Their prayers would bounce back in their faces as though there were an iron wall between them and heaven.

This symbolic act teaches an important spiritual principle. When a person continues to ignore God's warnings, there comes a time when it is too late to repent (Num. 14:39-45; Amos 4:6-12).

The years of punishment (4:4-8).—The Lord instructed Ezekiel to lie on his left side for 390 days to represent symbolically the number of years of punishment on Israel, the Northern Kingdom. Then the prophet was to lie on his right side for forty days to represent the number of years of punishment on Judah, the Southern Kingdom. He was to be bound with ropes while he performed this symbolic act so that he could not turn from side to side. It is not clear whether Ezekiel was actually bound during the entire 430 days or whether he repeated the symbolic act a portion of each day. The meaning of the act was clear, however. It warned of the years of punishment on Israel and Judah because of their faithlessness to the Lord.

The severity of the siege of Jerusalem (4:9-17).—Ezekiel was instructed to perform an additional symbolic act during the 390 days that he lay on his left side. The Lord instructed him to make bread from wheat, barley, beans, lentils, millet, and spelt (v. 9). Since bread was usually made from wheat alone, the use of coarser materials suggests that grain of all kinds was going to be very scarce during the siege (see also Deut. 22:9). The people would use whatever grain was available to bake their bread. It is unlikely that Ezekiel baked enough bread at one time for the entire 390 days. Therefore, it is better to assume that he was only tied a part of each day and was free the rest of the time to bake bread and to perform other duties.

To impress the people even more dramatically with the scarcity of food during the seige of Jerusalem, the Lord instructed Ezekiel to weigh the amount of food he would eat each day (v. 10). He was allowed twenty shekels a day, about nine ounces—a very meager diet! In addition, the water he was to drink each day was only one-sixth of a hin—less than a quart (v. 11). Ezekiel's warning about the severity of the siege of Jerusalem was all too accurate, for during the actual siege the people were reduced to cannibalism (see Jer. 19:9; Lam. 4:10).

Ezekiel was further instructed to bake the bread in the sight of the people, using dried human dung as fuel (v. 12). According to the Mosaic law, contact with human excrement made a person cere-monially unclean, that is, unfit to participate in the ritual worship practices prescribed by the law (Lev. 5:3; 7:21; Deut. 23:12-14). By baking the bread as he was commanded, Ezekiel was warning the people symbolically that the time was coming when they would be scattered among the nations and thereby become unclean. The reason that every foreign land was considered unclean (Amos 7:17) was because God was not worshiped there.

Ordinarily Ezekiel did not hesitate to do anything the Lord asked him to do, but on this one occasion he hesitated. The fuel to be used for cooking the bread created a dilemma for Ezekiel, for it would make him unclean. He reminded the Lord that he had never done anything deliberately that would make him unclean (v. 14). His priestly training could not be easily dismissed. The Lord modified his instruction in consideration for Ezekiel's scruples by allowing him to cook the bread over cow's dung (v. 15).

The meaning of this symbolic act could not have been misunder-stood by those who witnessed it. The Lord was warning that the time was coming when food and water would be so scarce in Jerusalem that it would have to be rationed during the siege.

A symbolic haircut (5:1-17).—In order to warn the people of the coming fate of Jerusalem, the Lord instructed Ezekiel to cut off all the hair on his head, including his beard. He was to divide the hair into three parts. One part was to be burned. Another part was to be tossed into the air and struck with a sword as the wind scattered it. The remaining part was to be scattered to the wind. A few hairs were to be bound in the skirt of Ezekiel's garment as assurance that a remnant would be spared. Even some of those hairs would be affected by the holocaust (vv. 3-4).

It must have been difficult for Ezekiel to bring himself to perform this symbolic act because of the dignity that was associated with a man's hair. Uncut hair was an evidence of a priest's consecration (Lev. 21:5). In ancient Israel it was a disgrace for any man's hair to be cut (2 Sam. 10:4-5). It was cut off only when a person was in mourning (Isa. 15:2) or had a skin disease (Lev. 13:29-37). Captives were humiliated by shaving their heads before leading them away as slaves. Cutting his hair would make Ezekiel an object of ridicule.

The meaning of this rather unusual symbolic act is clear. It anticipated the fate of the people during the siege of Jerusalem. One-third of them would die of pestilence and famine. A third would be killed by the enemy, and a third would be scattered to other nations, either in flight from the enemy or as captives. The fate of the devastated nation would make them "a reproach and a taunt, a warning and a horror" to other nations (v. 15). The certainty of Jerusalem's destruction is emphasized by the threefold repetition of "I, the Lord, have spoken" (vv. 13,15,17).

Warning of the Coming Punishment (6:1 to 7:27)

Israel was attracted to idolatrous worship practices very early in her history. The people worshiped idols during their years of bondage in Egypt (20:8). They were attracted to the immoral practices associated with Baal worship during the wilderness wanderings (Num. 25:1-5). They ignored Moses' warnings that the worship of their neighbors' gods would bring about their downfall (Deut. 4:15-28; 6:14-15). Ezekiel repeated the warning of earlier prophets that the people should destroy their idols or God would destroy the people and their idols.

A warning to the mountains (6:1-7).—The Lord instructed Ezekiel to proclaim a warning against the mountains of Israel. We, of course, understand that the mountains themselves were not the objects of God's wrath. It was the people, who built their high places and altars on the mountains for the worship of their deities, who would be punished. God warned that he was going to destroy the idolatrous places of worship and the people who worshiped there. Their dead bodies would surround the altars to which they would flee in the vain hope that their gods would protect them from the enemy. After the terrible slaughter, the survivors would then know who was truly the Lord (v. 7). God may be known in one of two ways—by faith or by experiencing his wrath. Judah had chosen the second way.

The promise of a remnant (6:8-10).—In spite of his anger with his people, God could not bring himself to destroy them completely (compare Hos. 11:8). After announcing judgment, he would frequently announce that he was going to spare some of the people. The Bible calls these survivors "the remnant" (for example, Amos 5:15; Isa. 10:20-22; Mic. 5:7-8; Zeph. 3:13). They would some day remember him in the faraway countries to which he had scattered them and form the nucleus of a restored people.

The Lord reminded the people of Judah that he had been deeply hurt by their sins (v. 9). The Hebrew of this verse says "I have been broken by their faithless heart." The Revised Standard Version translates it as "I have broken their wanton heart" and misses the point. (See RSV footnote.) No greater incentive can be discovered for abandoning our sins than the realization that God is deeply hurt when we sin (see Jer. 8:21). The Lord predicted that one day his people would loathe themselves for all the evil deeds they had committed (v. 9).

Another warning of punishment (6:11-14).—To show his distress over the wickedness of his people, Ezekiel was told to clap his hands and stamp his foot (v. 11). The Lord reminded him again of the destruction of the people by sword, famine, and pestilence. Their dead bodies would be scattered about on the mountains where they once had worshiped their idols. The devastation would extend to every corner of the nation from its southern extremity to its northern boundaries. Then they would know that the Lord was what he claimed to be. Unfortunately, they would not make that discovery until after Judah fell to the Babylonians.

Time has run out (7:1-4).—The messages of chapter 7 deliberately use repetitious words and phrases to emphasize the certainty of Judah's doom. They appear with the monotonous repetition of a hammer pounding nails: "An end! The end has come . . . Now the end" (vv. 2-3). "An end has come, the end has come; . . . it comes" (v. 6). The language of this chapter is strong, but God's judgment is never pleasant.

Time had run out for the people of Judah. True, the Lord is "merciful and gracious, slow to anger, and abounding in steadfast love" (Ex. 34:6), but his patience has limits. When they refused to listen to the warnings of prophets he had sent time after time, punishment had to come. God announced that the "end has come" for the entire nation (v. 2). Ezekiel spoke of the coming disaster as though it had already happened. Actually, Judah's "end" was still several years in the future, but it was as good as done since God said it would take place.

The Lord's anger was going to be unleashed against Judah like a wild beast turned loose against his helpless prey. He was going to judge them for what they had done and then punish them for all their abominable practices. Surely then they would know that he was the Lord (v. 4).

The announcement of doom by a wrathful God (7:5-13).—The prophets frequently emphasized their messages by a play on words which, of course, can only be seen in the Hebrew language in which the Old Testament was originally written. Ezekiel made a play on the sound of words in these verses. He announced in v. 6, "The end [a word that sounds like *haqqets* in Hebrew] . . . has awakened" (a word that sounds like *heqits* in Hebrew). Like a person waking from sleep, Judah's final destruction was awakening.

The people were accustomed to hearing the restrained shouts of the orgiastic rituals on the hillsides. Soon they were going to hear noise and shouting that would contain no mirth. Rather, the sounds would be the agonizing shrieks of a people experiencing the wrath of God poured out on them like molten metal (v. 8). With a warning that should have caused cold chills to go up and down their spines, the Lord announced that "my eye will not spare, nor will I have pity" (v. 9).

The Lord compared Judah's wickedness to a plant that has developed from a seed to a sprout and finally to a flower. Judah's injustice had blossomed, their pride had budded, and their violence had grown into a rod of wickedness (vv. 10-11). Therefore, their day of doom was rapidly approaching. Destruction would be complete. Their wealth would be taken from them. It was not a time for a buyer to rejoice that he had made a good purchase or for a seller to mourn that he had been forced to sell his property (v. 12). The point of this verse is that conditions would be so chaotic during the time of Judah's punishment that the normal practices associated with buying and selling would be suspended. Life as the people of Judah had known it was coming to an end.

According to the Mosaic law of the Jubilee of the land, any family property that had been sold by its owner had to be returned to that family during the Jubilee year that occurred every fifty years (Lev. 25:8-17). The law was designed to keep inherited land within a family. The Lord warned that the coming calamity would obliterate all titles and legitimate claims to family land. That generation would not see the reestablishment of the Mosaic regulations during their lifetime. Because of their wickedness, they would all die in their sins (v. 13).

The futility of resistance (7:14-23).—Ezekiel painted a bleak picture to counteract any false hope the people of Judah may have entertained about their ability to resist the enemy. Although they had sounded the trumpet to call the people to prepare for defense, all their efforts were going to be useless (v. 14). God himself was against them. The sword, pestilence, and famine would overwhelm them. Even those who escaped would be overcome with grief. Their wails would sound like the mournful sound made by doves. In their defeat they were going to be paralyzed by fear and helplessness. They would be as "weak as water" (v. 17). In accordance with the mourning practices of those times, the people would cover themselves with sackcloth and ashes and cut off their hair. Fear would be wrapped about them like a garment (v. 18).

The people of Judah were going to discover that their valued possessions, such as silver and gold, were worthless. Silver and gold could not be eaten. There would be no food available that wealth could purchase. Many people would throw their silver and gold into the streets as though it were worthless trash. Their wealth had been a stumbling block that caused them to sin (v. 19). They would discover that the idols they had made from their silver and gold were worthless when the enemy carried away their idols and other possessions as the spoils of war.

Ezekiel knew that some of them would turn in desperation to the Lord for help, but the Lord would turn his face away from them. Even his protecting presence would be removed from the Temple. It would be profaned and destroyed by the enemy. Later, Ezekiel describes the departure of God's glory from the Temple (11:22-23).

God's judgment on Judah's sins (7:24-27).—Because of their wickedness and violent deeds, God announced that he was going to use the "worst of the nations"—that is, Babylon—to destroy Judah and her Temple (v. 24). The people would seek peace but not find it. They would turn to their leaders for help but not find it. Prophet, priest, elder, and king were going to be overcome by despair. Everyone in the land would shake with terror.

By means of a reverse application of the Golden Rule (Matt. 7:12), the Lord announced that he was going to judge the people of Judah in the same way they had judged others (v. 27; compare Matt. 7:2). That announcement alone should have brought terror to the hearts of those people who had oppressed the poor, cheated the widows and orphans, and denied justice to the common people (compare Amos 4:1; 5:10-12; 8:4).

Ezekiel's Visit to Jerusalem in a Vision (8:1 to 11:25)

No other Old Testament prophet experienced so many visions as Ezekiel. Altogether, seventeen chapters of the book contain accounts of visions. Ezekiel's call in chapters 1—3 was a visionary experience. It is introduced by the words, "The heavens were opened, and I saw visions" (1:1). His best-known vision was of the valley of dry bones (37:1-14), and his vision of a restored Israel and a new Temple occupies the last nine chapters of the book (40:1 to 48:35). It is important to keep in mind that everything described in chapters 8—11 took place in a vision while Ezekiel was seated in his home with some elders. These men were leaders in exile and had probably come to Ezekiel either for advice or encouragement.

Abhorrent Worship Practices in the Temple (8:1-18)

It is difficult to understand how a people who had been so uniquely blessed by God could turn away from him and worship the local Canaanite deities. It is almost unbelievable that they brought these alien gods into the Temple of God in Jerusalem in open defiance of his command, "You shall have no other gods before me" (Ex. 20:3). The abominable worship practices in the Temple that are described in this chapter make it clear why God's judgment was about to fall on his people.

Date of the vision (8:1-4).—In the sixth year of Ezekiel's exile in Babylon, God appeared to the prophet again as he had at the river Chebar (8:2; compare 1:27). It was one year and two months after his first vision (1:1-2). The Spirit carried Ezekiel to the Temple, where he saw the idolatrous worship practices of his people conducted openly and without shame. These worship practices were provoking the anger of God.

Image worship that provoked God's jealousy (8:5-6).—North of the altar gate Ezekiel saw an "image of jealousy" at the gate's entrance. It was an image of an unnamed god that the people were worshiping inside the Temple area itself. It is called an "image of jealousy" because it was provoking God to jealousy (v. 3). The altar was the place where the blood was sprinkled as an act of worship of the Lord (Lev. 1:11). Now the sacred area was being desecrated by the idol that had been placed nearby.

"Jealousy" in the Old Testament comes from a word that means "the color produced in the face by deep emotion." The association between "jealousy" and "color produced in the face" can be explained by an illustration. If someone walked up to you and forcibly took a valuable possession from you, you would have an emotional reaction. Your face would become flushed with anger.

God's jealousy in relation to his people was like that. The Hebrew people belonged to God. He resented any efforts to draw the people's loyalty away from him. The fact that he reacted with "jealousy" to the enticement of an idol reveals just how valuable his people were to him (see Ex. 19:5; 1 Pet. 2:9). No reaction from God would have meant he didn't care about his people.

The jealousy of God is to be understood as one of his positive attributes, in the same category with love and compassion. It is not to be confused with our use of the word *jealousy* to describe the petty emotion associated with envy and suspicion.

Animal worship by the elders (8:7-13).—Ezekiel was then taken to a secret room in the Temple that was reached by digging through a hole in the wall. There he saw all kinds of animals drawn on the walls and seventy of the elders burning incense as an act of worship of the animals. Animals were commonly worshiped in the ancient world, especially in Egypt, but their worship was abhorrent to God. The elders knew that the worship of animals was forbidden and therefore worshiped them in secret. They justified what they were doing by accusing God of having forsaken the land. They believed an absentee God could not know what they were doing.

Tammuz worship by the women (8:14-15).—Again Ezekiel was taken to the entrance of the north gate of the Temple. There he saw women weeping for Tammuz, a Babylonian fertility deity. It was believed that Tammuz died at the end of the growing season in the fall. He went to the underworld where he remained until his "resurrection," which coincided with the beginning of spring. His "death" was observed by solemn rituals and much weeping. By worshiping Tammuz the women were declaring their belief that Tammuz, not God, was the source of their land's fertility.

Sun worship in the Temple (8:16-18).—Ezekiel was then taken to the inner court of the Temple. He saw about twenty-five men, probably priests, standing at the Temple door with their backs to the Temple. They were facing the sun in the east and putting a branch to the nose in some kind of act of worship of the sun. The sun was widely recognized as a deity in the ancient world. Re, the sun god, was a chief deity in Egypt. The people of Judah should have known better than to worship the sun. Their Scriptures clearly taught that the sun was created by God (Gen. 1). They had chosen to degrade themselves and to insult God by worshiping the created rather than the Creator (Rom. 1:18-25).

By showing Ezekiel what was taking place in the Temple, God was justifying the coming outpouring of his wrath on Judah. When that time came, he would have no pity on her inhabitants even when they cried out to him amidst the agony of the destruction of their nation.

Divine Executioners and a Mark of Protection (9:1-11)

Ezekiel's visionary experience in Jerusalem was not yet finished. The Lord wanted him to see the terrible slaughter that was about to be inflicted on the city.

The Lord called for the executioners of the city to assemble with their weapons for slaughter. Six men responded when he summoned and stood beside the bronze altar. They symbolized the divine judgment that was about to fall on Jerusalem. One of the men was clothed in linen and carried a case at his side that contained writing instruments (v. 2). God ordered him to go through Jerusalem and place a mark on the foreheads of all those who grieved over the wickedness being committed in Jerusalem (v. 4). Unfortunately, there were not enough righteous people like them in the city to avert its destruction. Centuries earlier, Sodom could have been saved if ten righteous people had lived in the city (Gen. 18:32; see also Jer. 5:1-5; Matt. 11:23-24).

In the ancient world, slaves were branded with a mark that identified their owner, as cattle are today. Worshipers of a deity frequently were branded or wore an emblem of identification to show which god they worshiped. The mark placed on those who grieved over Jerusalem's abominations would distinguish them as truly belonging to the Lord. It would protect them from the judgment that was about to fall on the rest of the people.

The Lord instructed the other men to begin their executions and to show no mercy. Young and old, including women and children, were to be slain. Only those who bore the protecting mark would be spared (v. 6). Judgment would begin at the Temple with the elders (see also Mal. 3:1-3; 1 Pet. 4:17).

Ezekiel could not bear to watch the terrible slaughter. He fell on his face and pleaded with God not to destroy the city entirely. It was too late, however, for a reprieve. The people's wickedness had sealed their fate. God's mercy is revealed whenever there is repentance, but there was no evidence of repentance in Jerusalem. Therefore, the Lord could only answer Ezekiel, "My eye will not spare, nor will I have pity" (v. 10). Then the man clothed in linen reported to the Lord that his commands had been carried out (v. 11).

The Fiery Destruction of the City (10:1-22)

Once again Ezekiel saw the throne that resembled a sapphire. It was on the platform that was above the heads of the cherubim (v. 1; see 1:26). He heard the Lord ordering the man clothed in linen to take the burning coals that the cherubim were transporting and to scatter them over Jerusalem (v. 2, Isa. 6:6).

The actual destruction of Jerusalem was accomplished by the Babylonian army, but this vision makes it clear that the destruction was divinely ordained. The Scriptures frequently speak of God using another nation as his instrument of judgment on his people (for example, Hos. 13:16; Amos 4:10; Hab. 1:6).

The glory of the Lord moved from where the cherubim were standing to the threshold of the Temple. The Temple was suddenly filled with a cloud, as it had been at its dedication by Solomon (1 Kings 8:10; see also Ex. 40:34; Hag. 2:7). The court was filled with the brightness of the Lord's glory, and Ezekiel could hear the sound of the cherubim's wings.

One of the cherubim took some of the fire that was between them and gave it to the man clothed in linen. Ezekiel peered intently at the cherubim. He observed the four wheels that looked like sparkling chrysolite (v. 9; see 1:16). There was one wheel beside each cherub, and a wheel within each wheel, that made it possible for the wheels to move in any direction without turning (v. 11).

Ezekiel noticed again that each cherub had four faces (v. 14). Thus, they, like the wheels, could move in any direction without turning. In 1:10 he described their four faces as those of a man, a lion, an ox, and an eagle. In verse 14 they are described as the face of a cherub, a man, a lion, and an eagle. He recognized them as the same living creatures he had seen by the river Chebar, though he did not call them cherubim at the first encounter (1:4-14).

Whenever the cherubim moved, the wheels moved. When the cherubim stood still, the wheels also stood still (v. 17; compare 1:21).

The glory of the Lord returned from the threshold of the Temple (see v. 4) and stood over the cherubim and then accompanied them to the door of the east gate of the Temple (v. 19).

The "glory" of the Lord is mentioned about nineteen times in Ezekiel. It can be defined as a manifestation of the presence of God and is frequently associated in the Scriptures with visible splendor and light. Moses asked to see God's glory (Ex. 33:18). When God revealed his glory to Moses, it is described in terms of God's attributes: "merciful and gracious, slow to anger" (Ex. 34:6). In the New Testament God's glory is linked to his Son: "The Word became flesh . . . we have beheld his glory, glory as of the only Son from the Father" (John 1:14).

God's Assurance in the Midst of Calamity (11:1-25)

The prophets did not speak only messages of doom and judgment. Neither did they speak only messages of hope and encouragement. They understood that God's word to his people included both judgment and hope. Before the fall of Jerusalem, Ezekiel's messages were mainly filled with warning of coming judgment. After its fall, he did not humiliate the people further by saying, "I told you so. You should have listened to me." Instead, he immediately changed his emphasis to one which would encourage the shattered nation that there was hope for the future.

God was not through with his covenant people. Even before Jerusalem fell, at the same time that he was warning of punishment, Ezekiel could speak of a future time when the people would walk obediently with God and experience his blessings.

Judgment on the wicked leaders (11:1-13).—Ezekiel's vision that began in 8:1 continues through chapter 11. He was taken by the Spirit to the east gate of the Temple (v. 1). There he saw twenty-five of the leaders. They should have had the best interests of the people at heart, but instead the Lord labeled the advice they were giving as "wicked" (v. 2). They were saying, "The time is not near to build houses; this city is the caldron, and we are the flesh" (v. 3). A modern equivalent of these pessimistic words might be, "Our goose is cooked!" However, the statement has also been interpreted as an expression of confidence that their strong fortifications would protect them like an iron caldron from the enemy. The verse could also be translated, "It is not near; let us build houses" (KJV). That would mean the leaders were giving the people false assurance that they were safe. They believed there was no danger from outside enemies, contrary to Ezekiel's warnings.

The Lord told Ezekiel to warn the people that their false hope was futile. Many of them who thought they were safe were going to be killed. Others would be taken captive and led away by the foreign conqueror who was God's instrument of judgment (v. 9). Those leaders who were giving false assurance that they were safe in the city would be among those led out of the land as captives. They would be judged far away from the city they had hoped would protect them (compare Jer. 39:5).

Even as Ezekiel spoke, Pelatiah, one of the twenty-five whom the prophet saw at the east gate, died (v. 13). Ezekiel was so shocked by the death of so eminent a leader that he questioned whether God was going to destroy even the remnant of the people (v. 13). Pelatiah's death may have been a symbolic warning of the coming fate of all the leaders or of the nation.

A promise of restoration (11:14-21).—Many of the people in Jerusalem assumed that God favored them over the exiles scattered among other nations. They thought the exiles were the ones who were being punished (v. 15; see also Jer. 24:1-10 for the same belief). The logic appeared to be sound, but it was wrong. The Lord indicated that he was protecting those who had been scattered. He would bring them together and return them to the land of Judah. Then they would form the nucleus of the restored nation. God called himself a "sanctuary" for the exiles (v. 16).

This remnant would enjoy a new relationship with the Lord. A time was coming when there would be no more idolatry in the land. The Lord was going to give the people one heart and a new spirit (v. 19). Their stony, obstinate hearts would be replaced by obedient hearts, sensitive and responsive to God's guidance. They would be the true covenant people of God, and God would acknowledge them as his people (v. 20). Ezekiel was speaking of a new relationship which Jeremiah described as a "new covenant" (Jer. 31:31) and which the New Testament describes as "be converted" (Acts 3:19, KJV; "turn again," RSV).

The departure of God's glory (11:22-25).—The women of Jerusalem had wept over the departure of Tammuz from their midst (8:14). They should have been weeping over the departure of God's glory, but they were not aware of his departure. The false prophets spoke a partial truth when they said that the people were safe with God's protecting presence in their midst (Jer. 7:4). They were giving the people a false sense of security, however, because they did not have the spiritual sensitivity to know that God's glory had departed.

Ezekiel saw God's glory leave the city and stand on the mountain (Mount of Olives?) east of the city. Later his glory would return by the same way it departed (43:1-4). Then the Spirit brought Ezekiel back to Chaldea, and so the vision came to an end. Ezekiel faithfully repeated to the exiles all he had been shown by the Lord in Jerusalem.

More Warnings of Coming Judgment (12:1 to 19:14)

Ezekiel still had not succeeded in getting his message across to the people of Judah that time was running out. He continued to warn them through symbolic acts, spoken parables, and mournful laments for the fate of their rulers.

Symbolic Acts to Warn of Jerusalem's Fall (12:1-28)

The Lord reminded Ezekiel that he lived among a rebellious people, "who have eyes to see, but see not, who have ears to hear, but hear not" (v. 2). Once again he instructed the prophet to perform a symbolic act to show them what was about to happen.

The fate of King Zedekiah (12:1-16).—Has the Lord ever asked you to do something that seemed so foolish it would cause people to talk or laugh at you? If so, you can understand how Ezekiel may have felt when the Lord asked him to dig a hole through a wall and pretend that he was fleeing a city under siege. He told Ezekiel to pack his baggage as if he were getting ready to go into exile. He was to put the baggage in front of his house in the daytime for all to see it. Then that night he was to come out of his house as though he were going away as an exile. He was instructed to dig through "the wall" in sight of the people (v. 5). The reference was probably to the wall of his house, as the Babylonian city walls were so thick that he could not possibly have dug through them. The inner city wall was twenty-one feet thick, and the outer wall was eleven feet thick. Nor is it likely that the Babylonians would have allowed him to damage their walls. Symbolically, he was showing the desperate measures that would be taken to escape from the Babylonians when Jerusalem was captured.

Ezekiel was further instructed to put his baggage on his shoulder and to cover his face as he walked away in the night (v. 6). The prophet carried out the symbolic act.

The next day the Lord told him to explain what he had done. The symbolic act was a warning to the king and the people in Jerusalem. The king would carry his own baggage as he attempted to escape through an opening that he had cleared away in the breached walls of Jerusalem. He would be captured, his eyes blinded, and he would be led away to Babylon, where he would die. All his supporters would be either killed by the sword or scattered among the nations (v. 14). Once again the Lord affirmed his intention to preserve a few of the people as a remnant who would one day repent and acknowledge that he was their God (v. 16).

Ezekiel's symbolic act was fulfilled when King Zedekiah attempted to escape from Jerusalem in the last days of the siege along with some of his followers. He was captured and brought before Nebuchadnezzar. He was forced to witness the execution of his own sons. Then he was blinded and led away in chains to Babylon (2 Kings 25:4-7; Jer. 39:4-7).

Horrors of the seige (12:17-20).—The Lord told Ezekiel to perform another symbolic act to impress upon the people the horrible fate that awaited Jerusalem. He instructed Ezekiel to shake and tremble as he ate his food and drank his water (v. 18). It was a visual attempt to show the terrible fear of the people during and after the siege of Jerusalem. They would be terrified when they saw their land despoiled and ruined by the enemy.

No further postponement of judgment (12:21-28).—Jeremiah warned of impending judgment for forty years before Judah was actually overrun by the Babylonians. Ezekiel gave similar warnings for over seven years. With each passing year that the prophets' dire warnings were not realized, the people became more confident that nothing was going to happen. They began to taunt the prophets with words like "The days grow long, and every vision comes to naught"

(v. 22) and "Where is the word of the Lord? Let it come!" (Jer. 17:15).

The Lord assured Ezekiel that he was soon going to put an end to their taunts and ridicule. The warnings of the prophet were about to be fulfilled. The groundless assurances and flattering words of false prophets were going to be exposed for the lies they were. God was going to carry out his word. Those who had laughed at the prophets would witness the destruction of the nation. Those who had scoffed that the prophets' warnings were for some far-off time were soon going to learn that there would be no further postponement of judgment for that generation.

Warnings Against False Prophets (13:1-23)

Much of the unwillingness of the people to listen to the prophets was due to the influence of their false prophets. There were men and women who claimed to be prophets and to be speaking for God the same as Jeremiah and Ezekiel. However, their words were always soothing and reassuring. They told the people what they wanted to hear—that everything was all right and that no calamity was going to overtake them. Ezekiel knew he must expose these people if he were to get a hearing for the Lord's word.

Foxes among the ruins (13:1-7).—The Lord commanded Ezekiel to speak out against the false prophets. Their messages were not from God but from their own minds. They spoke their own desires, for they had received no visions from the Lord. He called such people "foolish," for they were without spiritual perception or moral integrity (v. 3). The Lord accused them of being like foxes among the ruins. They were clever, destructive, and unscrupulous. They had not done anything constructive to prepare the people for the coming struggle. If they had been true prophets, they would have "gone up into the breaches" (v. 5), that is, they would have been calling the people back to God. They lied when they said, "Says the Lord" (v. 6), but they expected God to fulfill their lying words, anyway! In their arrogant self-deceit, they must have believed that they were true prophets.

Plasterers with whitewash (13:8-16).—The Lord made it clear that he was against those who had lied to the people and claimed to experience visions that in reality were only delusions. He would not acknowledge that such people belonged to him. They had no right to occupy positions of respect in the council of his people or to be enrolled in the register of true Israelites (v. 9). Moreover, they would not be allowed to return to the land of Judah.

Their assurances of "Peace" were misleading the people because only war and destruction awaited the nation. The Lord compared such people to a person who plasters over a wall with whitewash (v. 10). Such a wall may appear to be beautiful and sturdy, but when the storms and rain beat against it, the poorly-built wall will crumble and fall (compare the advice given in Matt. 7:24-27).

God's wrath was going to be poured out like a deluge of rain and a stormy wind (v. 13). Judah would crumble and fall like the whitewashed wall. The false prophets who lulled the people into a sense of false security by their lying words would also experience the wrath of God. They would be destroyed just like the whitewashed wall.

False prophetesses (13:17-23).—In ancient Israel the prophetic gift was not limited to men. Miriam (Ex. 15:20), Deborah (Judg. 4:4), Huldah (2 Kings 22:14), Noadiah (Neh. 6:14), Isaiah's wife (Isa. 8:3), and Anna (Luke 2:36) were called prophetesses. Just as there were true and false prophets, so there were true and false prophetesses.

Ezekiel had a word of warning for the women who "prophesy out of their own minds" (v. 17). He described some of the magical tricks they used to impress the people (v. 18). The exact manner in which they used the magic bands and veils is not known, but the purpose was to convince the people of their powers. They pronounced curses on those who opposed them and did whatever they could to dishearten their critics. Their blessings were reserved for those who paid them for their services (vv. 18-19). Out of superstitious fear many people had come under the control of the prophetesses and were being mercilessly exploited by them.

The Lord warned that he was opposed to their evil practices. He was going to break the hold they had over the people (v. 20). Their gullible victims would be released like the prey that is taken away from a wild beast. These false prophetesses had discouraged righteous people and encouraged wicked people, but their fate was sealed. The Lord was going to deliver his people out of their power. Then they would know that he was the Lord (v. 23).

Warnings Against Idolaters (14:1-23)

Idolatry seems to have been an ongoing problem among the people of Israel from their earliest history. Jacob found it necessary to cleanse his household of foreign gods (Gen. 35:2). His descendants worshiped idols during the years they spent in Egypt (Ezek. 20:8). After their deliverance from Egypt, they should have no longer been attracted to other gods. However, even before they reached the Promised Land, they began worshiping Baal (Num. 25:2-3) in spite of Moses' warnings (Deut. 6:14-15). King Solomon opened the floodgates for the worship of other gods in Israel by worshiping the gods of his wives (1 Kings 11:4). Ezekiel was not the first prophet to warn the people that their idolatrous worship practices would bring about the downfall of the nation.

Warning of punishment of idolaters (14:1-11).—While some of the elders were visiting Ezekiel, perhaps seeking a message from God, the Lord revealed to him that they were idol worshipers. It was an affront to God that they should consult him, but he gave them a message anyway. He instructed Ezekiel to warn them that their idols were stumbling blocks of iniquity (v. 4). If they did not repent and abandon their idols, they would die (vv. 6,8). The Hebrew of verse 8 says they would be "cut off" from their people. The phrase can refer to excommunication but here death is probably the intended meaning. The Lord warned that he would destroy the prophet who was deceived by the idols (v. 9). Punishment of the idolaters would be severe in order to serve as a warning to the people never to stray from God again.

It is a fact of history that although the Jewish people did not become wholly obedient after the punishment inflicted on them during the Exile, they apparently learned one lesson well. They did abandon their idols and were not attracted to them from that day to this.

Too late for righteous men to save Jerusalem (14:12-23).—The Lord wanted to impress upon Ezekiel how widespread was the wickedness in Judah. He said that even if Noah, Daniel, and Job— all noted for their righteousness (see Gen. 6:9; Dan. 6:23; Job 1:1,8)—were living in Jerusalem, their influence would not be sufficient to save the city or postpone its judgment. Their own lives would be spared (see 9:4-6), but their righteousness would not prevent the death of their own children or the desolation of the land. Centuries before, Sodom could have been spared if ten righteous people could have been found in the city (Gen. 18:32). Jerusalem apparently was more wicked than Sodom!

If Ezekiel could see what kind of people lived in Jerusalem, he would understand why God's judgment could not be averted. He would know that what God was doing was not without good reason (v. 23).

A question has been raised by scholars whether Daniel, who was a contemporary of Ezekiel living in Babylon at that time, could have gained such a reputation for righteousness as to be mentioned in the same breath with Noah and Job. Some scholars believe the Daniel mentioned here is a figure in Canaanite mythology who was known as a righteous judge for the cause of widows and orphans. This may be so, but it does seem strange that Ezekiel would include a mythological Daniel as an example of righteousness. It seems stranger that Ezekiel would include as an example of righteousness one who by his own definition could not be a righteous person. In 18:5-9 a righteous person is described as one who worships no god except the Lord. The Canaanite Daniel was not a worshiper of the Lord.

Several important lessons can be learned from these verses: (1) a righteous person is under God's protection; (2) that protection does not automatically extend to others; (3) each person is accountable before God; and (4) the influence of a sufficient number of righteous people can avert God's judgment.

Parable of a Worthless Vine (15:1-8)

A parable is a fictional story intended to teach a central moral or spiritual principle. Like Jesus the Old Testament prophets used parables as a means of communicating God's revelation (Hos. 12:10). The Lord asked Ezekiel to consider the wood of the grapevine. Its wood cannot be turned into furniture or other useful articles. It isn't even useful for making a peg to hang a pot on (v. 3)! If the wood of the vine is useless when whole, how much less use could be found for a piece pulled from the fire, burned at both ends and charred in the middle (v. 5)?

The Lord explained the parable to Ezekiel. The people of Jerusalem were like the wood of the grapevine, worthless to God because of their faithlessness. God was going to destroy his people like a useless vine tossed into the fire, because of their disloyalty to him.

Parable of an Unfaithful Wife (16:1-43)

In the Old Testament the faithlessness of Israel and Judah to God is frequently compared to a faithless wife. Hosea's marriage experience with a faithless wife became a kind of living parable through which that prophet learned the extent of God's love and forgiveness. Ezekiel's parable of an unfaithful wife describes faithless Judah in terms of three stages of life—infancy, marriage, and life after marriage. Some parts of the description are blunt and unpleasant to read, but sin is like that. It cannot be described with flattering words.

An abandoned baby (16:1-7).—The Lord traced the ancestry of the people of Jerusalem to the land of the Canaanites, where they had both Amorite and Hittite ancestors. No one nurtured or cared for the people who would become known as Israelites. They were like a baby who received no special attention at its birth. In ancient times a neglected, unloved newborn infant's navel cord was left uncut from the baby. She was not washed or rubbed with salt (which was applied for hygienic reasons) or wrapped in soft cloths. In the ancient world, unwanted babies, especially girls, were often abandoned to die or to be dragged away by wild animals. Before the Hebrew people made a covenant with God, no one cared for them. There is probably a comparison in these verses to the early struggle of the patriarchs and their families for survival in Canaan and to the years of bondage in Egypt.

Their chances for survival in Egypt were as slight as those of a baby abandoned by its parents. The pharaoh was determined to destroy them from the face of the earth. But God had not forgotten his people, and he protected them from annihilation. Like the abandoned baby that somehow survives and grows to adulthood (v. 7), so the Hebrew people survived the rigors of slavery in Egypt.

A chosen bride (16:8-14).—The parable now focuses upon the abandoned baby who has reached marriageable age. Like the man who falls in love with a maiden, marries her, and then tenderly takes care of her, so God compared his love for the people that no one else loved. He brought them out of Egypt and made a covenant with them at Mount Sinai. The covenant, which is the equivalent of marriage in the parable, was not made because of their greatness but because the Lord loved them (see Deut. 7:7-8). The people were chosen as God's bride by grace, a term that is frequently defined as "unmerited love."

Like the husband who delights to buy expensive clothing, jewelry, and finery of all kind for his bride, so God delighted in blessing his people with material abundance in the land he gave them (vv. 10-13).

Like the bride who develops into a dazzling beauty because of the attention and love lavished on her by her husband, so Israel became famous and wealthy among the nations (v. 14). This part of the parable corresponds to the early years of the monarchy under David and Solomon, when the hitherto insignificant people became an international power among the nations of the ancient world.

A faithless wife (16:15-34).—Like a beautiful wife who is flattered by the attention given her until she gives herself in an immoral relation to another man, so Israel broke the vows of faithfulness she had taken when she made a covenant with God at Mount Sinai. Her "lovers" were the gods of her neighbors to whom she gave herself. Her faithlessness to God was not a one-time occurrence. It eventually became a way of life until she lusted after the other gods like a prostitute after her lovers. She had no desire to give them up (see Jer. 18:12).

The people took their gold and silver, which had come to them through God's blessings, and made them into idols which they worshiped (v. 17; see Hos. 2:8). The embroidered garments they owned as a result of God's bounty were used to robe their idols. Oil and incense that should have been presented to the Lord were given to other gods. The fruits of the land that the people enjoyed as a result of God's favor—flour, oil, and honey—were offered to other gods (v. 19). They even sacrificed their children to the false gods (vv. 20-21). They did not remember the goodness of God or how he had brought them out of Egypt and blessed them (v. 22).

Their harlotries were political as well as religious. Instead of depending on God, they turned to the Egyptians, the Philistines (who were ashamed of the lewd behavior of the Israelites!), and the Assyrians (vv. 26-28). They were willing to make an alliance with any godless nation that approached them. The broken promises and mistreatment at the hands of those nations did not bring the covenant people to their senses. Some of them were even now turning to the Babylonians for help (v. 29).

Throughout these verses the Lord has been saying Judah was like a harlot, but now he has another thought. Judah is different from harlots (v. 34). Harlots give their services for money and gifts. Judah's alliances did not benefit her. Rather, she paid tribute money to those nations who were willing to make a treaty with her. Perhaps out of a desire for international recognition, Judah sought alliances with other nations, even though the alliances were not mutually beneficial.

A harlot's punishment (16:35-43).—According to law and custom in many ancient lands, a harlot or an adulterous wife was punished by public humiliation. She was forcibly brought out of her house, tried publicly, and condemned. Her clothing and jewels were stripped from her before the assembled crowd. Then she was stoned to death, and her body was cut to pieces. The house she lived in was burned. The women of the community were forced to watch the proceedings as a warning not to commit the same sin.

The meaning of this part of Ezekiel's parable is unmistakable. Judah was about to be punished like a faithless wife or harlot. None of her lovers (that is, allies) would come to her defense. She would be stripped of her wealth and destroyed. Then God's wrath would be satisfied.

Parable of Three Sisters (16:44-63)

These verses may be a continuation of the previous parable, as the underlying teaching is the same. However, the parable changes from the story of an abandoned baby who grew up to be an adored wife who forfeited her husband's love and devotion because she could not resist other lovers. Ezekiel now compares the history of the Jewish people to three sisters.

The Lord reminded the people of their pagan ancestry that included Hittites and Amorites. The people of Judah, like their ancestors, worshiped other gods, hence the proverb that would be used about them, "Like mother, like daughter" (v. 44).

Jerusalem had two "sisters." One of them was Samaria, the capital of the Northern Kingdom that was destroyed by the Assyrians in 722 BC (v. 46). The second was Sodom, destroyed during the time of Abraham because of its wickedness (Gen. 19:24-25).

Jerusalem should have learned some lessons from the fate of those two cities that were destroyed because of their wickedness, but she did not. Although Sodom was proud, luxury loving, and indifferent to the poor, the Lord said she was not as wicked as Jerusalem. Samaria had not committed half the sins that Jerusalem had. In comparison to the abominations committed by the people of Jerusalem, Sodom and Samaria appeared righteous (vv. 51-52)!

In an unusual reminder of God's grace, he promised to restore the fortunes of both Sodom and Samaria. The time would come when Jerusalem would be ashamed of her wickedness, and God would restore her, also (vv. 53-54).

Sodom had become synonymous with wickedness and total depravity for the people of Judah. The name itself was used as a byword in Jerusalem, but now Jerusalem was going to become the same kind of despised figure in the eyes of her neighbors, including the hated Edomites and Philistines (v. 57).

The parable concludes, not on a note of judgment, but with a word of hope, as do so many of the messages of Ezekiel and other prophets. After denouncing Judah for breaking the covenant, God acknowledged that he had not forgotten the covenant he made with them. They might be faithless to the covenant, but he could not act the same way. Therefore, the time is coming when he will establish an everlasting covenant with his people (this is the "new covenant" mentioned in Jer. 31:31). The people will be ashamed of their past faithlessness and ingratitude when they experience God's forgiveness and their restoration as a nation. The restored nation will include the land occupied by Samaria and Sodom. They will not be equal to Jerusalem but subject to her.

The underlying emphasis of the parables of this chapter is the forgetfulness of human beings and the faithfulness of God. People forget their earlier commitment to the Lord which is as binding as the vows of a marriage covenant. They forget the material and spiritual blessings of God, and also forget his warnings of punishment for disobedience. But God never forgets his covenant promises; he keeps his word. All people, like ancient Jerusalem, should be ashamed that they could experience God's grace regardless of what they may have done, but reject it.

Parable of Two Eagles (17:1-24)

Two eagles and a vine (17:1-10).—The Lord instructed Ezekiel to tell the people a parable about two great eagles. The first eagle came to Lebanon, broke off the top branch of a cedar, and carried it away to a city in another country. Then he took some seed of Lebanon and planted it in fertile soil where there was abundant water. The seed produced a luxuriant vine with branches that turned toward the eagle.

Then along came another great eagle, and the vine turned its roots and branches toward him. The eagle transplanted it in another place so it could thrive and produce fruit, but the Lord warned that he was going to uproot the vine so it would wither away.

Interpretation of the parable (17:11-21).—The Lord told Ezekiel to explain the parable to the rebellious people. The first eagle represented King Nebuchadnezzar, who took King Jehoiachin of Judah and other nobles to Babylon, "a city of merchants" (v. 4). He replaced Jehoiachin as king with another member of the royal family named Zedekiah. But the new king turned to Egypt for help against the Babylonians. The Lord warned that as punishment for not submitting to the Babylonians Zedekiah would die in Babylon (v. 16). Pharaoh's promised help would be insufficient to save the besieged city of Jerusalem from Nebuchadnezzar, and Zedekiah's troops would be scattered as refugees or prisoners. The warnings contained in the parable were literally fulfilled against Jehoiachin and Zedekiah. (See 2 Kings 24:12-15,17; 25:6-7; Jer. 37:5,7 for the fulfillment of Ezekiel's parable.)

Promise of a new ruler (17:22-24).—Continuing the figures used in the parable of two eagles, the Lord said that he was going to take a sprig from the top of a cedar and plant it on a lofty mountain. It would become a great cedar and bear fruit. Birds of every kind would take refuge in its shade. The other trees would know that it is the Lord who prospers them or causes them to wither.

These words have clear messianic implications. They suggest that since Judah's kings had failed to be the right kind of rulers, the Lord will provide his own king whom he will exalt. That king will prosper and provide security for those who seek refuge in him. God's sovereignty will eventually be acknowledged by all peoples because of the exaltation of this "tree." Christians see in these words a clear anticipation of the work and triumph of Jesus Christ.

Other passages in the Old Testament that use a "branch" of a tree as a messianic figure are Isaiah 11:1; Jeremiah 23:5; 33:15; and Daniel 11:7.

Sour Grapes and Children's Teeth (18:1-32)

No other prophets emphasize individual responsibility quite so much as Jeremiah and Ezekiel. For this reason, they have sometimes been called "the prophets of individualism." Both of them attacked a popular saying among the people which inferred that innocent people were punished for the sins of others (see Jer. 31:29-30). Both insisted that each individual is held accountable for his own sins.

Rejection of a popular saying (18:1-4).—The people of Judah had popular proverbs, just as we do. Such proverbs, or popular sayings, are intended to summarize what is believed to be true, based on common, tested experience. However, popular sayings sometimes prove to be false.

The Lord rebuked the people for saying, "The fathers have eaten sour grapes, and the children's teeth are set on edge" (v. 2). The proverb implied that previous generations had committed sins for which the present generation was being punished by an unjust God. It is no more possible that God would punish an innocent person for the sins of someone else than for one person to bite into a sour grape and hear a passerby complain that his teeth felt the acid of the sour fruit. Judah was trying to shift the blame for its sins, but God said, "The soul that sins shall die" (v. 4).

The righteous shall live (18:5-9).—Who was considered a righteous person in the Old Testament? In verses 5-9 Ezekiel gives one of the clearest answers to this question to be found in the Bible. A righteous person is one who does not worship idols or commit immoral acts and does not exploit anyone. In short, he keeps the laws of God, not to become righteous but because God's nature has already entered him through faith (Gen. 15:6). By keeping the law, he fulfills the requirements imposed on him by the covenant relationship and reflects God's own nature. That person will live (v. 9).

It is not clearly stated whether "live" means an abundant life now or eternal life. It may include both meanings, but the real comparison seems to be life and death in terms of God's favor and disfavor.

The wicked son of a righteous man shall die (18:10-13).—If a righteous man has a son who steals, kills, commits immoral acts, worships idols, and oppresses the poor, that son will die. The righteousness of one person cannot cover the wickedness of another. Each person is held responsible for his own acts.

Some insight into the contrast between *righteous* and *wicked* can be gained from the meaning of the Hebrew words. *Righteous* comes from a word that means "to be straight" or "firm." *Wicked* comes from a word that means "out of joint."

The righteous son of a wicked man shall live (18:14-20).—If the righteousness of a father cannot cover the wickedness of a son, the reverse is equally true. A righteous son is not held responsible for the sins of his father.

A wicked man who turns from his sins shall live (18:21-23).—A person who sees the error of his way of life and turns away from it is not chained by his past. Instead, that person's sins will not be held against him. God has no pleasure in bringing judgment and prefers that the wicked person turn from his sins and live.

A righteous man who turns from his righteousness shall die (18:24).—If a righteous person makes a complete change in the direction of his life and gives himself to wickedness as a way of life, his past goodness will not save him from punishment.

This verse might seem to contradict the New Testament teaching of the eternal security of the believer, but it does not. It is not dealing with the issue of eternal life or eternal damnation. It is an appeal to the people of Judah to live their covenant obligations. Obedience to the law set out in the covenant brought blessing; disobedience brought punishment (Deut. 28).

A defense of God's justice (18:25-29).—The people who heard Ezekiel's explanation of individual responsibility protested that the ways of the Lord were not just. The Lord rejected their complaint and responded that they were the ones who were not just! He affirmed again that a righteous person who commits sin will be punished and the wicked man who turns away from his wickedness will save his life.

In these verses God's judgment seems to be based solely on a person's actions, but what we do proceeds from an inner attitude toward God. A person's conduct reveals his true relationship with God, regardless of his pious words.

An appeal to live (18:30-32).—God's final word on his justice is that each person will be judged according to the kind of life he chooses. No one need be punished for sin; every person can choose to repent and turn from his life of wickedness. The person who turns away from his old life will receive a new heart and a new spirit (v. 31). The way of forgiveness is open to every person because God has no pleasure in the death of anyone.

Parables of a Lion and a Vine (19:1-14)

There is nothing more tragic than the person who has potential for greatness but who never becomes what he could have been because of wrong choices. He fails because he may have chosen not to submit to the discipline of study and preparation. He may have chosen self-destruction through the gratification of carnal desires by means of drugs, alcohol, or illicit sex. It may have been the rejection of the lordship of Christ over his life that caused him to fail. Some tragic figures in the Bible who failed to achieve their potential include Samson, Saul, and Judas Iscariot.

A comparison of Judah's rulers to a lion (19:1-9).—Ezekiel lamented the forfeited potential of the rulers of Judah. He compared them to the lion, an animal noted for its strength and courage. Like a lion captured in a pit and then led away in chains, King Jehoahaz was deposed by Pharaoh and taken as a prisoner to Egypt (v. 4; see 2 Kings 23:33-34).

The identity of the second lion is not so certain (vv. 5-9). Since Jehoiakim succeeded Jehoahaz as ruler and was a very strong king, verses 5-9 may refer to him. Like a caged lion (v. 9), Jehoiakim was taken as a captive to Babylon, but apparently was released and allowed to return to Jerusalem (2 Chron. 36:6; Dan. 1:1-2). Jehoiachin, Jehoiakim's successor, was taken prisoner to Babylon, but as he only ruled for three months, he could not have been the one who "laid waste their cities" (v. 7). Zedekiah succeeded Jehoiachin and was eventually taken as a prisoner to Babylon, so it is possible that the lament was for him.

There is another way to interpret these verses. Instead of trying to identify a particular ruler, the lions may represent a composite picture of the kings of Judah to show how they forfeited their power and to show their consequent fate.

A comparison of Judah's rulers to a vine (19:10-14).—In a comparison that sounds very much like the parable of the eagles in 17:1-10, Ezekiel compared Judah's rulers to a vine. The vine prospered and was fruitful (v. 10). It was exalted among the nations (v. 11). But in anger God ravaged the vine with a hot east wind and with fire. The vine was transplanted in a dry desert where it survived, but without fruit or strength.

The lament clearly reflects the coming destruction and captivity that Ezekiel foresaw. Ezekiel may have had in mind as the "vine" either Jehoiachin or Zedekiah, for both were carried away from Jerusalem as captives of Nebuchadnezzar.

Two important lessons are implied in Ezekiel's lament: (1) no nation can live on its past glory, and (2) nations fall because of the wrong kind of leaders.

Still More Warnings of Coming Judgment (20:1 to 24:27)

It had been seven years since Ezekiel had been taken to Babylon along with King Jehoiachin and other leaders. For two years since his call he had been warning the people of the coming judgment on Judah. No one listened, but he continued to plead with them.

History of a Rebellious People (20:1-44)

A review of past rebellions (20:1-31).—Certain elders came to Ezekiel to inquire of the Lord (see 8:1 and 14:1 for other visits by the elders). Apparently they recognized that Ezekiel was a prophet although they would not obey his advice. Because he knew their hearts, the Lord was angry that the elders wanted a word from him. He told Ezekiel to present a legal case against the people of Judah by reminding the elders of Judah's faithlessness that went back to the years spent in Egypt. God had ordered them in Egypt to give up their idols, but they refused (vv. 7-8).

He reminded the elders that instead of destroying them in Egypt because of their idolatry, he brought them out of that land (vv. 8-9). He made a covenant with them at Mount Sinai, and they freely agreed to the covenant terms. But they rebelled against the Lord during the years in the wilderness by breaking the laws of God (v. 13). The Lord recalled how in his anger he almost destroyed the people in the wilderness. He knew, however, that if he did not bring them into the Promised Land other nations would say it was because he did not have the power to complete the task (v. 22; Ex. 32:12). He did punish them, though, by allowing an entire generation to die in the wilderness before their children entered Canaan.

Unfortunately, the children did not profit from the punishment inflicted on their parents. They had the same rebellious spirit as their parents.

The Israelites had rebelled against God in Egypt and during the wilderness years. They continued to rebel against him even after he brought them into the Promised Land (vv. 27-31). They continued to worship other gods, even to the time of Ezekiel's generation. They

were offering gifts to other gods, including the sacrifice of their sons
by fire. The Lord said such people had forfeited their right to seek
guidance from him (v. 31).

In these brief verses Ezekiel summarized the history of Israel
from the years of bondage in Egypt to his own day. It can be
summarized in one phrase: a history of rebellion—rebellion in
Egypt, in the wilderness, and in the Promised Land.

A promise of future restoration (20:32-44).—In spite of an
unbroken history of rebellion, God had not given up on his people.
He was still determined to be acknowledged as their king (v. 33). To
bring this about would require punishment and purging of the
rebels. By scattering them among the nations, he was giving them
the freedom to worship their idols, but they would no longer
profane his name by worshiping their idols in Jerusalem (v. 39).

Those who survived the purging would form the remnant of a
restored community of worshipers. God was going to bring them
back where, after repentance, they would once again worship the
Lord acceptably. As a result of the years of punishment and the
subsequent restoration to their land, the people would finally know
that the Lord God was their God.

Judgment by Fire and Sword (20:45 to 21:32)

A fire kindled by God (20:45-49).—The Lord instructed Ezekiel
to "preach against the south, and prophesy against the forest land in
the Negeb" (v. 46). The geographical region in the southern part of
modern Israel is still known as the Negeb (also spelled Negev). The
Lord warned that his judgment would scorch the land of Judah like a
blazing fire that could not be extinguished.

Ezekiel knew the people would ridicule the warning as just
another of his harmless parables. They would mock him as a teller of
parables (v. 49). When people do not want to believe God's warnings
today, they, also, criticize the preacher who brings the warnings!

A sword unsheathed against Jerusalem (21:1-17).—The Lord told
Ezekiel to proclaim his hostility against Jerusalem and the land of
Judah. Like the warrior who draws his sword and starts cutting
down his enemy, God was going to slaughter the people in Judah.
He instructed Ezekiel to perform another symbolic act (see 4:1-3 for
Ezekiel's first symbolic act). The prophet was to groan aloud as
though his heart were breaking with grief (v. 6). When the people

asked him why he groaned, he was to tell them that it was because of the coming destruction of Jerusalem. The news of the disaster will melt the hearts of the exiles and cause their knees to be as weak as water. The vivid language describes the traumatic shock the exiles will experience when they learn of the destruction of their beloved city.

The sword is mentioned fifteen times in this chapter. Its frequent mention demonstrates that as Jerusalem's day of doom neared, Ezekiel's warnings became more intense. The Lord told Ezekiel to clap his hands and let the sword come down three times to mark the beginning of the great slaughter that was going to overtake the people (v. 14). He described it as a glittering sword, "made like lightning . . . polished for slaughter" (v. 15).

Nebuchadnezzar at the crossroads (21:18-23).—Ezekiel was instructed to perform yet another symbolic act. He was to set up a signpost at a crossroads with one signpost pointing to Jerusalem and the other pointing to Rabbah, the capital city of Ammon (v. 20). Rabbah is known today as Amman and is the capital of Jordan.

Nebuchadnezzar's army would soon move south through Syria toward Jerusalem. At a crossroads the superstitious king would resort to divination to determine whether he should proceed to Rabbah or to Jerusalem. The decision was so crucial that he would use several means of divination to ensure accuracy. He would shake some arrows marked with the names of the cities and then draw one, just as some people today draw straws to make decisions. He would also consult stone or clay representations of household gods (known as teraphim) and would also examine the markings on animal livers for guidance.

All the signs would point to Jerusalem as the city to be attacked first by the invading Babylonian army. Ezekiel's symbolic act at the crossroads should have convinced the people that judgment was coming soon, but they dismissed it as false divination (v. 23).

The fate of King Zedekiah of Judah (21:24-27).—The Lord sent a warning to King Zedekiah that because he had sinned openly his day of punishment was at hand. His crown would be taken from him as an act of humiliation. God was going to exalt that which was low and abase that which was high (v. 26; see also Matt. 23:12). Not a trace of the ruins of Jerusalem would remain "until he comes whose right it is" (v. 27). These words echo the blessing pronounced on Judah by his dying father Jacob: "The scepter shall not depart from Judah . . .

until he comes to whom it belongs" (Gen. 49:10; the KJV says, " . . . until Shiloh comes"). The words speak of a coming ruler through the family of Judah and are therefore to be understood as messianic.

The fate of the Ammonites (21:28-32).—Although Nebuchadnezzar chose to attack Jerusalem first, it did not mean that the Ammonites would escape his fury. The sword was going to fall on them, also. They would suffer a bloody destruction and be forgotten as a nation (v. 32).

God's Accusation Against His People (22:1-31)

Like the prosecuting attorney in court who brings formal charges against the accused, the Lord described the sins of Judah that would result in her punishment.

Bloodshed upon a shedder of blood (22:1-16).—The prophet Nahum had referred to the godless city of Nineveh as a "bloody city" (Nah. 3:1). Ezekiel applied the same words to Jerusalem (v. 2). He was instructed to declare openly all the abominable deeds of the city. The time for reckoning had come for a city that had worshiped idols and had shed much blood, perhaps a reference to human sacrifice for religious purposes (v. 3). Her guilt concerning these sins was bringing the day of judgment closer and closer. When her punishment comes, God will not spare her from the humiliating jeers and taunts of other nations.

The Lord then turned his attention to the leaders for a special word of rebuke. The Scriptures frequently single out the leaders as objects of God's wrath (for example, Hos. 4:4-10; Amos 2:3; Zeph. 3:3-4). Judah's leaders abused their power, shed blood, and mistreated parents, orphans, and widows. They broke the sabbath laws and worshiped idols. They committed all kinds of immoral acts, including incest and adultery. They became wealthy at the expense of their neighbors. Their indifferent attitude toward God's laws showed that they had forgotten him (v. 12). Forgetting God is the beginning of all sin.

The Lord dared the corrupt leaders to continue to be arrogant and bold in the day when he began to deal with them. He warned that he was going to scatter them among the nations and consume their filthiness like a purging fire. Through their ordeal, they would come to know that he was the Lord (v. 16).

Refining in the furnace (22:17-22).—The Lord compared the coming punishment of Judah to the refining of metal. (See also

Isa. 1:22,25; 48:10; Jer. 6:27-30; 9:7; Zech. 13:9; Mal. 3:2, where this same figure is used.) Impure metals are refined by subjecting them to intense heat. In the molten state the impurities rise to the top and are skimmed off, leaving the pure metal. Jerusalem's fiery destruction would serve as the furnace for a people who had become to the Lord like a mixture of impure metals.

There may not be a message of hope contained in these words, as was true in 15:1-8. Ordinarily, the figure of the refining of metal suggests that a purified remnant will remain, but here the message closes only with the statement that like metal that is melted in a furnace, the wicked people of Jerusalem will be "melted" (v. 22). This interpretation agrees with statements elsewhere that say God will restore Israel through the exiles, not through those in Jerusalem (see Jer. 24:1-10).

Accusation against all the people in Jerusalem (22:23-31).—In these verses the Lord's condemnation expanded to include all the people in Jerusalem, not just the leaders. True, their prophets and princes were like wild beasts, killing and robbing the defenseless for their own dishonest gain (vv. 25,27). The priests were also equally guilty. They violated the law and ignored the distinctions between the holy and the common. They failed to teach the people the law and disregarded the sabbath (v. 26; see also Mal. 1:6 to 2:9). The prophets whitewashed the seriousness of the situation with their false visions and lying words that they claimed were from the Lord (v. 28; see also 13:1-16).

The common people were not guiltless, however. They, like their leaders, robbed and oppressed those weaker than themselves. The Lord looked in vain for a single person to stand in the breach for him in order that he might spare Jerusalem, but he found no one (v. 30; the same idea is expressed in 13:5 and Jer. 5:1-6). These words may contain an allusion to Moses, who stood in the breach for his people (Ps. 106:23). There was nothing to be done except to let God's fiery wrath be poured out on them like molten metal (v. 31).

Parable of Two Sisters (23:1-49)

Ezekiel resorted to another parable to try to convince Judah of the enormity of her faithlessness. This parable is similar in some respects to the parable of three sisters (see 16:39-63). Some of the descriptive language is blunt, as it was in the other parable.

Identification of the sisters (23:1-4).—In this parable Ezekiel introduces two sisters named Oholah and Oholibah. He identifies them as the daughters of one mother. In daring language God described them as harlots who became his wives. According to the law in Leviticus 18:18, a man was forbidden to marry sisters, but this is a parable.

Oholah ("Aholah", KJV; the name means "her tent") is identified as Samaria, destroyed by the Assyrians in 722 BC. The other sister is Oholibah ("Aholibah", KJV; the name means "my tent in her"). This name suggests that the legitimate Temple was in Jerusalem and not at the rival shrines of Dan and Bethel in the Northern Kingdom of Israel (1 Kings 12:26-30). Oholibah represents Jerusalem, soon to face destruction at the hands of the Babylonians.

Alliances of Oholah and her punishment (23:5-10).—Oholah (that is, Samaria) was faithless to God even though she claimed to have a covenant relationship with him. Like the prostitute who gives herself freely to the soldiers of an army, so Samaria sought to please the Assyrians. She gave herself over to the worship of the Assyrian gods, as well as holding on to her idols she had worshiped since her years of bondage in Egypt. She thought she could save herself by making friends with the Assyrians, but she was wrong. The Assyrians had no regard for Samaria. They destroyed the beautiful city with its ivory-paneled homes after a three-year siege, ravaging the people and the land, because it suited their imperialistic ambition.

The "harlotry" of Oholah was political, religious, and physical. As judgment for their faithlessness, God gave Samaria and the Northern Kingdom of Israel over to the Assyrians.

Alliances of Oholibah and her punishment (23:11-35).—The Lord described Oholibah (that is, Jerusalem) as more corrupt than her sister. Oholibah should have learned some lessons from her sister's fate, but she did not. She defiled herself in the same way with the Assyrians as her sister had done. The practices involved in the reference to "men portrayed upon the wall" are unknown (vv. 14-15). They may have included some kind of abhorrent immorality, for the Lord said that "she carried her harlotry further" than Oholah (v. 14).

Oholibah polluted herself with the Babylonians, also. Her immorality was so openly flaunted that the Lord turned away in disgust (v. 18). She returned to the same kind of immorality she had practiced in Egypt. The Lord had once described Israel as a silly dove, first going to Egypt and then to Assyria for help (Hos. 7:11). Judah was now doing the same thing, first with Assyria and then with Babylonia.

The Lord warned Oholibah that he was going to incite an attack against her by her "lovers" (v. 22; the nations she had turned to for help). The invaders would include Pekod, Shoa, and Koa, nomadic tribes living east of the Tigris River who allied themselves with the Babylonians and Chaldeans (v. 23).

The enemy would come against Jerusalem from the north, although Babylon lay to the east of Jerusalem (v. 24). East to west travel would have required marching through a forbidding desert region, so armies from Mesopotamia followed the Euphrates River in their military campaigns against the west. This route brought them to Syria, which lay to the north of Israel. This meant that any invasion of Israel or Judah by Assyria or Babylon would come from the north.

The Revised Standard Version follows the Septuagint (Greek) translation with its translation "from the north." The Hebrew word for "from the north" is not found anywhere else in the Old Testament, and its actual meaning is somewhat uncertain. The King James Version translates it as "with chariots"; the New American Standard Bible and New International Version translate it as "with weapons." Whatever the exact meaning of this particular word may be, the entire verse describes a mighty army that will overrun Judah.

The fury and horror of the invasion is described with sickening realism in verses 25-26. The population of Jerusalem will be mutilated and slaughtered, the women will be raped, and the city will be looted. The punishment will be so severe that Jerusalem will never again dare to worship idols or turn to the Egyptians for help (v. 27). But the people could blame no one except themselves (v. 30). They were being punished for their idolatry, described in these verses as harlotry, lewdness, and pollution.

Oholibah's punishment is then described as her sister's cup which she must drink (vv. 32-34). Called here "a cup of horror and desolation" (v. 33), it is the cup of God's wrath described in Jeremiah 25:15-29. The probable origin of the "cup" to represent God's judgment is found in Numbers 5:11-31, which describes a potion a wife was required to drink if she were suspected of being unfaithful to her husband. The "cup" is also mentioned in Psalm 75:8; Isaiah 51:17; Habbakuk 2:16; Lamentations 4:21; Zechariah 12:2; Mark 10:38; and Revelation 14:10. When Jesus prayed that the cup might pass from him, he undoubtedly was thinking of the cup in the Old Testament as a symbol of God's wrath (Mark 14:36; Luke 22:42).

God's judgment on the two sisters (23:36-49).—The Lord asked Ezekiel to set out the legal case against both sisters (v. 36). He enumerated some of their sins: idolatry, human sacrifice to other gods, defilement of the Temple, breaking of the sabbath laws, and religious orgies to which foreigners were invited. On the same day that they slaughtered their children for their gods, they also came into the Temple to worship the Lord (v. 39)!

Because the two sisters were acting like adulteresses, they were going to be punished like adulteresses—by stoning to death (Lev. 20:10; Deut. 22:21-24). The "stoning" in this case would actually be the enemy's sword that the Lord was sending against them. Thus, God would put an end to their religious harlotry, and they would acknowledge that he was the Lord God (v. 49).

Parable of a Rusty Cooking Pot (24:1-14)

Unlike other parables of Ezekiel, this one is dated. It was on the tenth day of the tenth month of the ninth year of Ezekiel's exile (v. 1). The date coincided with the beginning of the siege of Jerusalem by Nebuchadnezzar's armies in 588 BC, a siege that lasted eighteen months (2 Kings 25:1; Jer. 39:1).

The parable (24:1-5).—The parable describes a rusty cooking pot in which choice pieces of meat have been placed that is set on a fire for cooking. The fire is made hot in order to boil the meat. The pieces of meat are removed from the pot indiscriminately.

Interpretation of the parable (24:6-14).—This parable differs from the usual form of a parable in that it continues in verses 6-14, interspersed at the same time with its interpretation. The command is given to heap on more fuel until the flesh is well boiled and even the bones are burned up. Then the empty pot is left on the fire to try to melt the rust in the intense heat, but it is to no avail. The rust cannot be removed.

The rusty cooking pot of this parable represents Jerusalem. The choice pieces of meat represent the leaders who are going to be punished for their wickedness. The fire represents the fiery destruction of Jerusalem to be inflicted by the Babylonians. The rust that cannot be removed represents the sin that clings to the wicked city in spite of previous punishment. The Lord will not hold back the severity of his punishment, for the people have brought it upon themselves.

The Unexpected Death of Ezekiel's Wife (24:15-27)

The verses that follow contain the most difficult symbolic act that Ezekiel was asked to perform. His wife was going to die, and the Lord ordered him not to mourn or to weep for her.

A difficult command (24:15-18).—The siege of Jerusalem had already begun (see 24:2) when the Lord told Ezekiel that his wife was going to die suddenly. The prophet was ordered not to weep or to give any indication that he was in mourning. Instead of removing his turban and his shoes as a mourner usually did, he was to keep them on. He was not to cover his face with a mourner's veil or to eat the customary funeral meal with his friends and relatives (see also Jer. 16:5-7 for reference to this custom).

The evening of that same day Ezekiel's wife died, and the next morning he carried out the Lord's instructions. In this symbolic act we see more clearly than in any other performed by Ezekiel the incredible self-discipline and obedience of this prophet. Ezekiel loved his wife dearly—she was "the delight" of his eyes (v. 16). It must have been almost unbearable not to express his grief.

More than any other Old Testament person, Ezekiel exemplifies the injunction of the apostle Paul: "Take every thought captive to obey Christ" (2 Cor. 10:5). Ezekiel's experience is a reminder that one called by God must surrender his private life to the Lord and that sometimes personal tragedy prepares us for effective service.

Interpretation of Ezekiel's behavior (24:19-24).—The Jewish exiles in Babylon must have been mystified by Ezekiel's stoic attitude toward his wife's death. So they asked him the meaning of his strange behavior. He told them that just as his wife had unexpectedly died so the Temple, "the pride of your power, the delight of your eyes" (v. 21), was going to be destroyed. Their relatives left behind in Jerusalem were going to be killed, also.

Then Ezekiel told the exiles to follow his example. As he had not openly mourned for his wife's death, so they were to make no outbursts when they learned of the destruction of Jerusalem.

Some scholars believe that Ezekiel's advice was for the protection of the exiles. If they openly lamented the destruction of Jerusalem, their Babylonian masters might be offended and retaliate against them, for it would be a joyful time for the victors.

It is more likely that the real reason the exiles were to show no grief was to reflect God's attitude toward the fall of Jerusalem. He had warned many times through the prophets that his patience was coming to an end. Because they had rejected every appeal to repent and thereby escape punishment, he would show no compassion when they cried out to him from the ruins of Jerusalem (see Jer. 11:14; 14:11-21; 15:1; Ezek. 7:4 for similar expressions of God's attitude).

A promise to Ezekiel (24:25-27).—The Lord informed Ezekiel that on the day of a fugitive's arrival in Babylon with news of Jerusalem's fall, the dumbness that had been imposed on him would be lifted (see 3:26-27). At least one good thing would come from Jerusalem's calamity. Ezekiel would be able to speak freely again! From the time of his call until the news of Jerusalem's fall reached Babylon, the only words Ezekiel spoke were messages given him by the Lord.

Messages of Judgment Against Other Nations
25:1 to 32:32

All the prophets with the exception of Hosea proclaimed messages of judgment against the nations around Israel and Judah. The most extensive collections of these messages are found in Amos 1—2; Isaiah 13—23; Zephaniah 2; Jeremiah 46—51; and Ezekiel 25—32.

The messages of judgment against other nations were no more severe than those directed against Israel and Judah. God was not blind to the sins of Israel and Judah or prejudiced against their neighbors. He is the righteous "Judge of all the earth" (Gen. 18:25) and punishes wickedness wherever he finds it.

By announcing judgment on the enemies of Israel or Judah, a prophet would receive a sympathetic hearing from the Hebrew people. Having gotten their attention, he was then able to launch into a judgment speech against them, as Amos did in Amos 1—2.

However, it would be demeaning to say the judgment messages against other nations only served as attention getters. They were authentic pronouncements of judgment against those nations. They also brought comfort to the Israelites in times of oppression by their enemies by reminding them that God does not let evil go unpunished. They received assurance by these messages that they would eventually be delivered from their godless oppressors.

A more important purpose served by these messages was to warn Judah and Israel that they could not escape God's judgment. If nations that did not know God came under his judgment, how much more could the covenant people expect to be punished for their sins?

Although the messages against other nations comprise a considerable part of the Old Testament prophetic books, Bible students usually pass over them very quickly. Most of them are about little-known nations, whereas our interest is centered in Israel. Also, they tend to make us uncomfortable by their vengeful spirit which seems to conflict with the New Testament emphasis on love and forgiveness.

Although it is easy to ignore the prophets' judgment messages against other nations, they should be carefully studied because they contain important theological principles. For example, by reminding us that no nation can escape God's judgment, they teach the universal sovereignty of God. They also teach that God may use one nation to execute judgment on another nation. Finally, they imply that the moral laws of God are binding on all nations; otherwise he would not punish pagan nations for breaking his laws.

Ezekiel's messages of judgment include seven foreign countries. The nation we would most expect to be included, Babylon, is not mentioned in these chapters, except as God's instrument of judgment on other nations!

In each of Ezekiel's judgment messages a nation is named and one of its sins is singled out for condemnation. Then the nature of the punishment is described, and finally, in some cases, the agent of judgment is named.

Judgment Against Ammon (25:1-7)

The Old Testament traces the origin of the Ammonites to the incestuous drunken orgy of Lot with his daughters. From that shameful episode Ammon was born to the younger daughter (Gen. 19:30-38). The Ammonites were a Semitic people who spoke a language very much like Hebrew. They occupied a geographical area north of Moab and northeast of the Dead Sea. Their capital was Rabbah, known in New Testament times as Philadelphia. They had a long history of hostility to Israel (for examples see Judg. 11; 1 Sam. 11:1-2; 2 Sam. 10:3-5).

The Ammonites' sin was their rejoicing over the fall of Israel and Judah (v. 3). They were going to be destroyed (v. 7). Their land would be occupied by nomadic tribes of the desert, called here "the people of the East" (v. 4). Josephus says that Nebuchadnezzar sent an army against Ammon and Moab in 582 and devastated the area. He probably ordered a deportation for Ammon similar to that already carried out in Judah in 587. The vacuum created by the sudden end of the Ammonite civilization allowed the nomads to pour into the region, as Ezekiel had predicted.

Judgment Against Moab (25:8-11)

The origin of the Moabites is traced to the same incestuous drunken orgy that resulted in Ammon's procreation (see 25:1-7). Moab was born to Lot's elder daughter (Gen. 19:30-38). The Moabites occupied a geographical area immediately east of the Dead Sea. Their hostility toward Israel dates back to the time of Moses and Balak (Num. 22—24). The Israelites were introduced to Baal worship for the first time by Moabite women (Num. 25:1-3). The Israelites were under Moabite control for eighteen years during the period of the judges (Judg. 3:12-30).

While David was a fugitive from Saul, he entrusted his parents to the safekeeping of the king of Moab (1 Sam. 22:3-4); but he later conquered Moab (2 Sam. 8:2), and it remained under Israelite control during the reign of Solomon. Mesha, King of Moab, regained Moabite independence after the death of King Ahab of Israel (2 Kings 3:5-27). His account of that struggle is recorded on a stone called the Mesha Stele that was found in 1868.

Moab's sin was her refusal to recognize the uniqueness of Judah among the nations (v. 8). Her punishment was the same as Ammon's. The nation was going to be destroyed and would be occupied by the nomadic "people of the East" (v. 10).

Judgment Against Edom (25:12-14)

Genesis 36:1 links the origin of the Edomites to Esau. They occupied an area south and east of Judah and the Dead Sea. They are mentioned frequently in the Bible, particularly as enemies of Judah (for example, 1 Sam. 14:47; 2 Sam. 8:13-14; 2 Kings 8:20-22; 14:7).

The Edomites submitted peaceably to the Babylonian yoke and joined the Babylonian forces in the conquest of Jerusalem in 587 (Lam. 4:21-22; Obad. 10-16). By the fourth century BC an Arab people called the Nabateans had occupied much of the Edomite territory and made Petra their capital. The Idumeans of New Testament times were descendants of the Edomites. King Herod, who sought to put Jesus to death, was an Idumean.

Edom's sin was her spiteful actions against Judah (v. 12). As punishment, the nation would be destroyed from one end to the other—that is, from the city of Teman in the north to the city of Dedan in the south (v. 13). God's instrument of judgment against the Edomites would be the Israelites (v. 14).

Judgment Against Philistia (25:15-17)

Historians generally agree that the Philistines originated in the Aegean region. In Egyptian records they were one of the "People of the Sea" who invaded Egypt about 1188 BC, but they were driven out by Ramses III. They settled along the eastern Mediterranean coast and proved to be a continual thorn in the side to the Israelites until they were subdued by David (2 Sam. 8:1). Ironically, the territorial name *Palestine* comes from the name *Philistine*.

The sin for which the Philistines were condemned was their premeditated, malicious vengeance against Judah (v. 15). As punishment the nation would be destroyed (v. 16). The enemy agent of destruction is not named, but Nebuchadnezzar subjugated the Philistines in 604, bringing to an end the influence of Philistine culture in the ancient world.

Judgment Against Tyre (26:1 to 28:19)

The Fall of Tyre (26:1-21)

Ezekiel's first dated message against other nations was pronounced against Tyre. It was the "eleventh year," the year Jerusalem fell (v. 1). Tyre was an important Phoenician city located on a small, rocky island about one-half mile from the Mediterranean mainland and twenty-five miles south of Sidon. Its excellent harbor made it a prosperous commercial center.

Tyre had a long and significant history dating back to perhaps 2800 BC. Its main harbor was built in the tenth century by Solomon's contemporary, King Hiram. It was besieged by the Assyrians in 727 for five years without being taken. It was besieged by the Babylonians for thirteen years before surrendering in 572. Alexander the Great connected the island to the mainland by hauling in dirt and rocks in order to move his war machines and troops against the city walls for attack. He took the city after only seven months. Tyre remained a center of commerce and industry in the Roman period. The natural advantage that protected it from enemies and its wealth gained from its trade made Tyre a proud city.

God's judgment on Tyre (26:1-6).—In the longest message delivered by any prophet against Tyre, Ezekiel pronounced judgment on the city because she had rejoiced over the fall of Jerusalem as a commercial competitor to the aggressive Tyrians (v. 2). He warned that God was going to send other nations against Tyre like the successive waves of the sea dashing against a rock (v. 3). The great city would be destroyed and become a place fit only for fishermen to spread their nets to dry (v. 5).

Nebuchadnezzar's attack on Tyre (26:7-14).—Ezekiel described in vivid detail the coming attack on Tyre by Nebuchadnezzar (sometimes, as here, spelled Nebuchadrezzar in the Old Testament). The Babylonians would besiege the city with great numbers of chariots, horsemen, and soldiers until it surrendered. The Tyrians living on the adjoining mainland would be killed, as well as those on the island. When the enemy entered the city, they would despoil it and kill its inhabitants. The sound of music and merrymaking would be heard no more in its streets and homes. The actual siege by Babylon lasted for thirteen years before Tyre finally surrendered.

Lament of other rulers (26:15-18).—Ezekiel warned that the news of the fall of such a great city was going to bring fear and trembling to Tyre's neighbors. The rulers of the neighboring lands (called "princes of the sea," v. 16) will show their sorrow in the customary way by removing their ornate garments and sitting upon the ground. They will lament the fate of the once renowned city. Tyre's power had once caused other people to tremble. Now these same people will tremble when they learn of Tyre's fall (vv. 17-18).

Tyre's dreadful end (26:19-21).—The Lord declared that when Tyre is laid waste, the waters of the sea will cover it. Not a trace of the once-proud city will remain. Its inhabitants will descend to the Pit. The Pit, or Sheol as it is sometimes called in Scriptures (see 1 Kings 2:6; Job 17:16), was believed in ancient times to be the dwelling place of the dead. It was a dreary, lifeless place for those departing from this life.

A Lament over Tyre (27:1-36)

The Lord instructed Ezekiel to offer a lament for the great commercial city. Tyre is described in these verses as a great merchant ship, like those that plied the waters of the Mediterranean in ancient times. Like one of these ships, Tyre boasted that she was "perfect in beauty" (v. 3).

Comparison of Tyre to a merchant ship (27:1-9a).—These verses provide an invaluable description of shipbuilding and commerce in ancient times, although they are intended primarily to describe the magnificence and power of Tyre. Ancient shipbuilders took pride in constructing their magnificent sailing boats. They brought fir trees from Senir (the Amorite name for Mount Hermon; see Deut. 3:9) to make the siding for the boat called Tyre. Lebanon's famed cedars were used for making her masts (v. 5). Oaks of Bashan (located east of the Jordan River) were used for oars because of the natural strength of this wood. The boat's decks were made of pine from Cyprus and inlaid with ivory. Sails were made of the finest embroidered linen from Egypt, and coverings were made of blue and purple from Elishah (location uncertain, perhaps another name for Cyprus). The materials used for the boat suggest luxury and royal splendor.

Rowers from Sidon and Arvard (located to the north of Tyre) were hired, as well as skillful pilots who had the ability to guide the boat away from dangerous waters. Elders and skilled craftsmen from Gebal (near modern Beirut and later known as Byblos) caulked the seams to make the boat seaworthy.

Tyre's international appeal (27:9b-25a).—The figure now appears to change from Tyre as a great sailing boat under construction to a literal description of Tyre as a great commercial city.

Ships came from everywhere to barter for the wares of Tyre (v. 9b). Other nations provided the mercenary soldiers needed by the city for her protection (vv. 10-11). These soldiers added to the impressive splendor of the city. They were stationed on the city walls and in the towers located on the walls.

Verses 12-25 contain a list of the many countries and cities which sent their ships and merchants to Tyre to exchange their products for the sought-after wares of Tyre. They brought silver, iron, bronze, and other metals. Slaves, animals, ivory, fabrics, grain, and other foods, wine, spices, and precious stones were among the many things bartered for the products of Tyre.

Wrecking of a mighty ship (27:25b-36).—In verses 9b-25a the description of Tyre was literal, but in verses 25b-36, Ezekiel returns to the comparison of Tyre as a mighty ship that has now been wrecked. Everyone associated with the boat, including builders, pilots, soldiers, and merchants will share in Tyre's loss, just as all those on board a sinking ship lose their lives.

Others not so closely associated with Tyre will mourn its destruction like those standing on the shore who watch helplessly as a great sailing vessel sinks. The mourning practices observed for a person's death will also be observed for the death of Tyre. These practices included casting dust and ashes on the head, shaving the hair, and covering oneself with sackcloth (v. 30).

Tyre's neighbors will grieve because they will no longer have access to the coveted goods from Tyre that they had once enjoyed. Part of their grief will be caused by their inability to understand why mighty Tyre should be destroyed (v. 32). Tyre's neighbors will be paralyzed with fear that the same thing could happen to them. Merchants will hiss when they come near the ruins of Tyre to express their astonishment or derision over the destruction of the once-proud city.

Perhaps the most important lesson that can be learned from Tyre's downfall is that wealth and power without God do not make a great nation.

A Message for the Ruler of Tyre (28:1-19)

In these verses the metaphor of a ship is abandoned. The Lord told Ezekiel to announce judgment on the ruler of Tyre. Some scholars believe the ruler described is Ithobaal II, who ruled Tyre from 574 to 564. However, the unidentified ruler may only be a figure for Tyre itself. In any case the meaning of the message is quite clear.

The ruler's sin (28:1-5).—Tyre's ruler became so proud that he vainly imagined he was a god (v. 2; see also Acts 12:20-23). He believed he was wiser than Daniel (v. 3; see 14:14 for the discussion of the identity of Daniel in Ezekiel). It was true that his knowledge and cleverness were responsible for his great wealth, but he became proud and took credit for his wealth. (See Deut. 8:17; Hos. 12:8; Dan. 4:30; Luke 12:15-21 for similar warnings.)

Judgment on the ruler (28:6-10).—Because the conceit of Tyre's ruler convinced him he was as wise as a god, the Lord determined to humble him (see Prov. 16:18; 29:23; Jas. 4:6).

The Lord declared that he was going to bring enemies against Tyre to kill the proud ruler and destroy his splendor. He will die as surely as men drown on a ship sinking in the open sea, and then he will descend to the Pit (v. 8; see 26:20 for the meaning of this word).

When the proud ruler finds himself conquered by those about to slay him, he will be questioned whether he still believes he is a god! His mortality at the hands of his slayers will prove he is a man and not a god. In perhaps the most humiliating taunt that could be hurled at another person, the ruler was warned that he was going to die the death of the uncircumcised at the hands of foreigners (v. 10). "Death of the uncircumcised" meant a dishonorable death and the denial of funeral honors.

Lamentation for the ruler (28:11-19).—The lament in these verses abounds in allusions to the Creation story in Genesis 1—3. It should be carefully observed that the lament is addressed to the king of Tyre (v. 12). Beyond that, the words are difficult to associate with Tyre's king except in the most figurative way. He is described as being in Eden and robed with all kinds of precious stones (v. 13). He was placed on the holy mountain of God along with an anointed cherub. He was blameless from the time of his creation until he became proud of his beauty and splendor. When he sinned, God cast him out of his mountain and destroyed him with fire until nothing but ashes remained.

There are four ways of interpreting 28:1-19: (1) it describes judgment on the king of Tyre or Tyre itself in highly figurative language drawn from a paradise story that was widely known in the ancient Near East; (2) it is intended to give the reader an account of the literal history of the fall of Satan, even though he is called a man in verses 2 and 9; (3) by use of subtle irony it is intended to suggest that the king of Tyre was a kind of satanic person; or (4) it is intended to parallel the fall of the king of Tyre or Tyre itself with the fall of Adam.

However the details of these verses are interpreted, it should be remembered above all else that Ezekiel had the judgment of Tyre uppermost in his mind. It should also be admitted that the language is highly figurative and that there are obscurities and difficulties with any interpretation proposed. There are also some parallels with Isaiah 14:4-21 that should be examined.

Whichever of the four interpretations is accepted, there are two facts upon which every one can agree: (1) the words make use of a paradise story, well known even to the Tyrians, else the message of warning would have been meaningless to them; and (2) the lament contains a solemn warning against pride.

Judgment Against Sidon (28:20-23)

Tyre and Sidon were so closely linked geographically and historically that some scholars believe 28:20-23 should be understood as an extension of the message against Tyre.

Sidon was a very ancient city on the Mediterranean coast with a good harbor. It was located about twenty-five miles north of Tyre and was a rival of Tyre, although Tyre was more powerful in Ezekiel's time. It was controlled at different times by Egypt, Assyria, Babylon, Persia, and Greece. Its influence continued into New Testament times.

Sidon's sin is not named, but verse 24 suggests one sin was Sidon's contempt for Israel. Its punishment would be destruction through pestilence and war (v. 23). The enemy is not named, but Sidon suffered conquest more than once during her long history.

Parenthetical: Restoration of Israel (28:24-26)

In these verses Ezekiel departed from his succession of judgment messages against other nations to insert a word of hope for Israel. Such a word was surely needed at the very time Jerusalem was destroyed. The Lord assured his people that a time was coming when they would no longer be afflicted by their neighbors (v. 24). The Lord will regather them to the land that he gave to Jacob (v. 25), and they will dwell securely in it because God will bring judgment on their neighbors who had treated them with contempt.

Judgment Against Egypt (29:1 to 32:32)

Ezekiel's longest judgment message was addressed to the Egyptians. There are actually seven messages in these chapters, and each one is dated except the third (30:1-19). The latest of all Ezekiel's dated messages is found in these chapters. The "twenty-seventh" year of 29:17 would be 571 BC. There is no way to ascertain how much longer Ezekiel continued his ministry after 571 BC.

The pattern of the announcement of judgment against Egypt is the same as the other judgment messages of Ezekiel. A sin is named, punishment is described, and the agent of punishment is sometimes indicated. Egypt's principal sin was her pride (see 29:3; 31:10). Her punishment was to be defeat by an enemy (29:4-5) but not total destruction. The message contains a promise of future restoration (29:13-16). Jeremiah also held out a word of hope for Egypt (Jer. 46:26). God's agent of punishment would be Babylon (29:19; 30:10; 32:11), a prediction that was fulfilled when Nebuchadnezzar invaded Egypt in 568 BC.

Egypt's history as a world power is usually considered to have begun around 2900 BC with the unification of Upper and Lower Egypt under Menes, who established the first dynasty, although her civilization began centuries before that. Altogether, thirty dynasties occupied the throne of Egypt until the time of Alexander the Great, when the Ptolemies, a Greek dynasty, assumed the rule of Egypt from 306 to 30 BC. The scientific, cultural, and political achievements of the Egyptians remain one of the most fascinating stories in the history of civilizations.

Egypt was never the great power after 1100 BC that she had been earlier, but she continued to entertain her delusions of her former splendor. By Ezekiel's time her attempts to be "Number One" were futile. Ezekiel described her as a clumsy monster (29:3), a broken reed (29:6-9a), as helpless as a person with broken arms (30:20-26), and as a once-great tree that had been chopped down (31:1-18).

A Warning to Pharaoh (29:1-16)

The Egyptian rulers were called pharaohs (the word means *great house*). They were believed by their people to be gods and therefore had unlimited power and authority over their subjects. The pharaoh addressed in these chapters was Apries, also called Hophra, who ruled Egypt from 589 to 570 BC. He is the one who encouraged Judah to rebel against Nebuchadnezzar by promising military aid. He kept his word and sent an army to the assistance of Jerusalem, but Nebuchadnezzar drove him away without much effort (Jer. 37:5-8).

Fate of the great monster (29:1-5).—This first message against Egypt was in the "tenth year in the tenth month." It was a year after Jerusalem's siege had begun and seven months before its fall (which occurred in the fifth month of the eleventh year of King Jehoiachin's exile, Jer. 52:12).

The message was addressed to Pharaoh Hophra. He is compared to a clumsy crocodile in the Nile River. Deluded by the egotistical belief that he was a god, he claimed credit for making the Nile. As punishment for attempting to usurp God's role as Creator, his fate is described in terms of a crocodile captured by hooks in its jaws and dragged away to the dry ground to die and to be devoured by vultures. Hophra was killed in his unsuccessful attempt to keep his throne from falling into the hands of a relative named Amasis, thus fulfilling Ezekiel's prophecy.

A broken reed (29:6-9a).—Hophra was then compared to a marsh reed that broke when Judah leaned on Egypt for help. Egypt had a well-deserved reputation for unreliability. She made promises that she could not keep. The papyrus reed was an appropriate figure for Egypt, as it grew in such abundance along the Nile.

Forty years of punishment (29:9b-16).—As punishment for Pharaoh's pretensions to deity, God said he was going to make the land desolate for forty years and scatter her people among the nations.

Egypt was not to share the fate of other nations that were

destroyed and never revived, such as Edom (see Mal. 1:3-4). Her punishment was to last forty years (v. 12). God promised to restore the nation afterwards, but it would only be a lowly kingdom, never again able to exalt itself above the other nations. The Israelites would never again turn to the Egyptians for help against an enemy.

The forty years mentioned in these verses coincide approximately with the reign of Nebuchadnezzar who proved his superiority over the Egyptians at the battle of Carchemish in 605 and again when he invaded Egypt in 568.

Nebuchadnezzar's Defeat of Egypt (29:17-21)

As previously noted, verses 17-21 contain the latest of Ezekiel's dated messages. It was the first day in 571 BC (v. 17). Mention is made of Nebuchadnezzar's expensive and largely unsuccessful campaign against Tyre. In return for the thirteen years of men and resources expended in the siege of Tyre, he received very little recompense by way of booty. Apparently the Tyrians were able to remove their valuables from the city during the years of siege. We have an idiom to describe hard work: "He worked his fingers to the bones." Ezekiel's equivalent was "Every head was made bald and every shoulder was rubbed bare" (v. 18).

However, the Lord said Nebuchadnezzar would be recompensed for his conquest of Egypt. The plunder of Egypt would be the wages for his army. Egypt's riches would go to Nebuchadnezzar as recompense for being God's instrument of judgment against Tyre (v. 20).

Chapter 29 closes with an obscure reference to a horn that will spring forth to the house of Israel. The horn is a frequent symbol for power in the Old Testament. The verse has been interpreted as a reference to the coming Messiah and also as a general reference to a future restoration of Israel.

The Coming Day of Judgment of Egypt (30:1-19)

A day of doom (30:1-9).—This chapter contains an undated message that begins with a call to wail because the day of the Lord was near. "The day of the Lord" is a phrase found twenty-nine times in the prophetic books (three of them in Ezekiel). The idea is also expressed other ways: "In that day" (Isa. 2:20); "in the latter days" (Dan. 10:14); "days are coming" (Jer. 49:2). It refers to the time in history when God will act to vindicate himself.

The Day of the Lord will be experienced universally because God is sovereign over all nations (Obad. 15). It will be a time of judgment of the wicked and vindication of the faithful (Isa. 13:6; Mal. 4:1-3). Accompanied by cosmic upheavals (Joel 2:31), a better world will finally emerge. The "new" world will be characterized by the transformation of nature (Amos 9:13; Zech. 14:6-7), of relations between man and his environment (Isa. 11:6-8), and of human relationships (Mic. 4:3). Zion (better known as Jerusalem) will be exalted among the nations (Zech. 14:16). In the Old Testament the Day of the Lord is spoken of as near at hand (Isa. 13:6) in the same way that the New Testament speaks of the imminence of the second coming of Christ. The final and climactic fulfillment of the Day of the Lord is described in the Book of Revelation.

Not only will Egypt experience the wrath of God in that day, but so will her allies—Ethiopia, Put, Lud, Arabia, and Libya (v. 5). All who support Egypt will fall with her. Her land and her cities will be laid waste from Migdol to Syene, that is, from one end of the country to the other. Then they will know that he is the Lord.

A day of defeat (30:10-12).—For the second time (see 29:19-20) Nebuchadnezzar is named as the one who will execute judgment on Egypt. There will be a great slaughter among the population, and the Lord will "dry up the Nile" (v. 12). The phrase describes the most terrible calamity that could come to Egypt—famine as a result of the failure of the water supply. Whereas other nations might depend on rain for the growing of crops, the Egyptians had the dependable annual flooding of the Nile and available water for irrigation at all times. Failure of the Nile was unthinkable to them.

A day of desolation (30:13-19).—The description of the thoroughness of Egypt's punishment continues in these verses. Her idols (the Hebrew word used here means "things of nothing") will be destroyed (v. 13). The pharaoh will be overthrown, and fear will grip all the land.

Egypt was proud of her great cities such as Pathros (the capital of upper Egypt), Zoan (also called Tanis), Thebes (modern Luxor and Karnak), and Pelusium. The walls of these and other cities will be broken down (vv. 14-16). The cities will be burned, and their inhabitants, including young men and women, will be killed by the enemy's sword. The proud might of Egypt will come to an end as the smoke of the burning cities covers the land (v. 18).

Pharaoh's Broken Arms (30:20-26)

Pharaoh Hophra had promised assistance to Judah if she would rebel against King Nebuchadnezzar. Thus encouraged, King Zedekiah stopped paying tribute to Babylon, and Nebuchadnezzar quickly sent an army to put down the rebellion. While Nebuchadnezzar had Jerusalem under siege, Hophra kept his word by sending an army to the assistance of the people of Jerusalem. The army was too weak to be effective, and Nebuchadnezzar lifted the siege only long enough to rout the Egyptians (Jer. 37:5-8).

The Lord spoke to Ezekiel in verses 20-26 against the background of Jerusalem's siege that began in 588 and Hophra's futile gesture of help. He compared the Egyptian king's weakness to a man with a broken arm. Furthermore, he was going to break Pharaoh's other arm; that is, he was going to make him totally helpless so that he could not hold a sword or offer any kind of military resistance to the Babylonians.

In contrast to the "broken arms" of Pharaoh, God said he was going to strengthen the arms of Babylon's king and put a sword in his hand to be used against Egypt. Many Egyptians would flee to other lands to escape Babylon's wrath.

Parable of a Great Cedar (31:1-18)

In previous warnings to Judah, Ezekiel compared her to a useless vine, a faithless wife, and a wayward sister (15:1-8; 16:1-63; 23:1-49). He compared Tyre to a ship (ch. 27). Now he delivers another message of judgment against Egypt, comparing her to a great cedar.

Egypt as a great cedar (31:1-9).—The Hebrew of verse 3 reads that "Assyria was a cedar in Lebanon." Because the verses that precede and follow are about Egypt, the Revised Standard Version modifies verse 3 to read "I will liken you to a cedar in Lebanon" so that it also describes Egypt. However, there is no need to change the text. Ezekiel was deliberately comparing another great cedar that had fallen—Assyria—to show that the same fate awaited proud Egypt. Lebanon was famous in the ancient world for her cedars that were eagerly sought by other nations as a choice building material.

Egypt's prosperity was like a tall and stately cedar with thick branches. Nourished by nearby waters, such a tree would tower above the other trees in the forest. Birds would seek refuge in its branches and make their nests there. Animals would seek shelter under it. Even the trees in the Garden of Eden could not compare with the beauty of such a tree (vv. 8-9)! Verse 9 contains a subtle teaching that whatever prosperity the wicked enjoy is due to the goodness and mercy of God, for it says God made Egypt beautiful.

The meaning of the parable is clear. Egypt was a glorious nation. Her wealth and the greatness of her achievements dazzled the rest of the ancient world. For centuries no other nation rivaled her in power, and many of them became Egyptian vassals.

Egypt as a fallen cedar (31:10-18).—Because of her haughtiness and her wickedness, Egypt was about to be punished. Earlier, Ezekiel had named Babylon as God's avenging executioner. However, in these verses Babylon is identified only as "the most terrible of the nations" (v. 12). Like the woodcutter who chops down a tree in the forest, so this powerful foe will "chop down" Egypt. Like the animals and the birds that flee from a falling tree, so the nations will abandon their alliances with Egypt.

The once mighty nation was destined for death and the Pit (v. 14; see 26:20 for a discussion of the Pit). Verse 15 employs another commonly used designation for the dwelling place of the dead. It calls that place "Sheol." "Sheol" comes from a word that means *to ask* and probably preserves a trace of an earlier belief that a person could get in touch with a dead person to ask advice of him. (For example, Saul consulted Samuel about the outcome of a battle with the Philistines, 1 Sam. 28:6-19).

Other nations will mourn the fall of Egypt. They will be afraid because they do not understand how mighty Egypt could have fallen. However, in spite of her past greatness and glory Egypt was no better than any other nation. If the trees in the Garden of Eden cannot avoid withering away and dying, then Egypt cannot escape her fate. In her degradation she will not be able to maintain her former aloof separateness from other nations. At one period in Egypt's history no daughter of a pharaoh was allowed to marry a foreign king, however great and powerful that king might be. No one but a member of Egyptian royalty was good enough for a pharaoh's daughter! The fact that Solomon married a pharaoh's daughter reveals the decline of Egypt in the tenth century BC (1 Kings 3:1). Egypt will not be able to avoid alliances with the uncircumcised and will be as unclean as a person who has touched a corpse (v. 18; see Num. 19:11).

Although verses 10-18 seem to speak of trees going to Sheol, it is obvious that the details of the parable should not be pressed that literally. The purpose is to show the fate of the pharaoh and the mighty Egyptian empire. Like the dead person who makes his abode in Sheol, so the pharaoh and the empire will die and be forgotten. Even though the message was intended primarily to announce the doom of Egypt, it incidentally gives some valuable information about the ancient belief in Sheol as the abode of the dead.

Lament for a Great Monster (32:1-16)

A year and nine months had passed since the message was proclaimed against Egypt that began in 31:1. It was now more than a year and a half since Jerusalem's fall to Babylon.

Slaying of the monster (32:1-8).—In words similar to the description of the pharaoh in 29:3-5, he is again compared to a clumsy crocodile, although he would have preferred being compared to a young lion (v. 2). The Hebrew word is *tannin* and refers to any large sea creature. The Revised Standard Version translation of "dragon" is improper, as it suggests a mythological fire-breathing creature. The monster described in these verses is clearly a crocodile, native to the waters of the Nile. Like a crocodile captured and dragged to dry land to die and to be eaten by the birds and animals, so the pharaoh will meet his fate. His death will be accompanied by unusual cosmic upheavals (vv. 7-8). The language used in these verses is intentionally bloody and violent to stress the enormity of the pharaoh's wickedness.

Nebuchadnezzar as the hunter (32:9-16).—Once again the king of Babylon is named as the enemy who will come against the pharaoh, as a hunter stalks a crocodile. Many Egyptians will perish, and the proud nation will be humbled. The desolation of the land is compared to a deserted watering place for cattle, no longer muddied by the feet of the animals seeking refreshment (vv. 13-14).

Ezekiel's lament for Egypt in verses 2-15 will be picked up by other nations and repeated by them (v. 16).

Egypt's Descent to the Underworld (32:17-32)

In the parable of a great cedar (see 31:1-18), Egypt's punishment was described in terms of a descent into Sheol, the abode of the dead (see 31:15; also called the Pit). Chapter 32, verses 17-32 continues the same thought but abandons the metaphor of a cedar. Ezekiel spoke this message in the same year as his lament for a great monster (v. 17; compare 32:1).

Egypt's destruction will be as humiliating as the burial of a circumcised person beside an uncircumcised one. In Sheol the Egyptians will find other formerly great kings and peoples. The verses remind the reader that history is filled with the rise and fall of great nations.

Among the nations who share the fate of the fallen empire of Egypt are Assyria (vv. 22-23), Elam (vv. 24-25; an important power bordering Assyria and Persia), Meshech and Tubal (vv. 26-28; these were tribes in Asia Minor), Edom (v. 29; see 25:12-14), rulers of the Syrian states north of Israel, and Sidon (v. 30).

Pharaoh will join this crowd of "has-been" powers and will get some kind of perverse comfort by knowing that his was not the only great world empire that perished (v. 31).

There are some important lessons that can be learned from a study of the messages against Egypt: (1) a nation, church, or individual can lose spiritual power through sin and not be aware of that loss (compare Judg. 16:20); (2) through pride people can develop a false sense of their own importance; (3) all earthly powers are powerless before God; and (4) all nations that resist God must be prepared to face his judgment.

Messages Concerning Israel's Restoration
33:1 to 39:29

The fall of Jerusalem marks a turning point in Ezekiel's prophetic ministry. Beginning with chapter 33 there is a noticeable shift in the tone of his messages. From the time of his call at the river Chebar until the fall of Jerusalem, his messages had largely been concerned with a warning of coming judgment on Judah. However, his warnings had gone unheeded, and Jerusalem suffered a devastation from which she would not recover for years.

It would have been tempting for a prophet who had been vindicated by the fulfillment of his warnings to spend the rest of his life gloating, "I told you so. You should have listened to me." Instead, Ezekiel's ministry shifted to one of encouragement and assurance that Judah was going to be restored. The book closes with a description of a magnificent new Temple and a renewed people living under the protection and blessings of God.

Ezekiel's Renewed Responsibilities as a Prophet (33:1-20)

Ezekiel's task was not completed with the fall of Jerusalem. He had earlier been commissioned as a watchman (see the discussion of the watchman in 3:17-21), and although his warnings to the people had been ignored, he continued warning them of danger to the nation. The Lord told him a second time that he was a watchman for the house of Israel (v. 7).

A Renewed Call to Be a Watchman (33:1-9)

One commentator said dramatically that "after thirty-two blood-soaked chapters, we come finally to the positive message" of the book. It is true that Ezekiel mentions blood more than any other prophet. The word is found about thirty times in chapters 1—32. However, it is found six times in chapter 33 and about fourteen times in the remaining fifteen chapters, called the "positive message."

Ezekiel also used the word *sword* over eighty times, more than any other prophet; about fourteen occurrences of the word are in chapters 33—48. The continued use of words like *blood* and *sword* show that it is a mistake to say that Ezekiel spoke *only* comforting words in chapters 33—48.

In verses 2-6 the responsibilities of a leader chosen by the people are compared to the duties of a watchman. Perhaps the comparison was intended as a rebuke to Judah's leaders who ignored the approaching danger and failed to warn their people. King Zedekiah was that kind of leader. Instead of encouraging the people to believe Jeremiah's warnings, he did what he could to keep Jeremiah's words from being publicized. Once he threatened the prophet, "Let no one know of these words and you shall not die" (Jer. 38:24).

Verses 7-9 are directed specifically to Ezekiel as the Lord's watchman. He was told that if he did not warn the wicked to turn from their ways, their blood would be required at his hand. The verses make it clear that God holds his servants accountable for the messages he gives them to proclaim.

A Renewed Appeal for Repentance (33:10-20)

In chapter 33 Ezekiel raises two concerns he has previously expressed: (1) the responsibility of the watchman to warn and (2) an individual's responsibility for his own sins (see 3:17-21 and 18:1-29). It is not accidental that the two concerns are linked together here, for they teach that responsibility is a two-way street. The watchman was required to give warning, but he was not responsible for obtaining a favorable response to the warning. Expressed in today's terms, the Christian has a responsibility to witness and to warn, but he is not responsible for results. Every individual is held accountable for his own sins.

There are five principal words for sin in the Old Testament: (1) *transgression*, that comes from a word meaning "to rebel"; (2) *iniquity*, from a word that means "to be twisted" or "distorted"; (3) *sin*, from a word that means "to miss the mark"; (4) *wickedness*, from a word that means "out of joint"; and (5) *evil*, from a word whose original meaning is not known. The words do not have identical meanings in the Hebrew language, as appears to be the case in English. They reflect different facets of the nature of sin as understood by the Hebrew people. Two of these words, "transgression" and "sins" are used in verse 10.

Some of the people of Judah must have been convicted by Ezekiel's warnings, at least sufficiently to ask, "How then can we live?" (v. 10). God assured them that he had no pleasure in the death of the wicked, and therefore he had provided a way to escape punishment for their sins. That way was to "turn back from your evil ways" (v. 11). This is the Hebrew way of saying, "Repent." The word, occurring seven times in this chapter, describes a person who is going in the wrong direction and deliberately changes his course.

Chapter 33, verses 10-20 is essentially a repetition of chapter 18. Once again Ezekiel explained that no one is bound by his past. When a righteous person sins, his past righteousness does not automatically cover that sin. It must be dealt with—by confession, according to the New Testament (1 John 1:9).

Verse 13 contains a warning that if a righteous person sins, people will not remember his past goodness. They will only remember his sins. He will become a reproach to his faith, for an unbelieving world is quick to stamp "hypocrite" on all believers when one of them stumbles. The other side of the coin is equally true. When a person turns from his sins and demonstrates by his changed life that he has abandoned his old ways, God forgets his past way of life, and people are eventually convinced that his changed life is genuine.

Ezekiel's words should not be interpreted to mean that a person is judged as to whether he is saved or lost solely on the basis of what he is doing at the very moment of death. The people of Judah objected to Ezekiel's teachings about individual responsibility for sin and accused the Lord of not being just. The term "just" here comes from the idea of weighing on scales. The people were saying God's scales were not adjusted to the right standard to give an honest measurement, that he was using crooked scales! God's response was to reaffirm that he "will judge each of you according to his ways" (v. 20).

News of Jerusalem's Fall Reaches Babylon (33:21-29)

The Arrival of a Fugitive from Jerusalem (33:21-22)

In the tenth month of the twelfth year of Ezekiel's exile a man who had escaped from Jerusalem arrived in Babylon with news that the city had fallen (v. 21). As Jerusalem had fallen in the fourth month of the eleventh year (see Jer. 39:2), it seems strange that it would have taken a year and a half for the news to reach Babylon.

Various solutions have been proposed to explain the unusual length of time required for the fugitive's journey. Some scholars emend the word "twelfth" year to read "eleventh," which would mean that it took only six months, rather than a year and six months, for the news to reach Babylon. Even that would seem to be a long time; for Ezra required only four months to make the same journey (Ezra 7:8-9). Others have suggested that different calendars were used in Babylon and Judah to calculate the months.

There is a more obvious solution. The Lord had told Ezekiel earlier that when a fugitive arrived from Jerusalem with news of its fall, he would speak and no longer be dumb (24:27). News of Jerusalem's fall had surely already reached Babylon, since we assume that King Zedekiah, along with over eight hundred other prisoners, was taken to Babylon soon after his capture (Jer. 52:29; 2 Kings 25:7). However, the first Jewish eyewitness to its fall, other than the captives, did not arrive until a year and a half later. The Babylonians were hunting out and killing or enslaving everyone who tried to escape Jerusalem. It would have been difficult for survivors to leave Judah undetected. Also, Babylon was probably the last place most of the survivors thought of going! It is not unreasonable to conclude that the first actual Jewish eyewitness to Jerusalem's fall did not arrive in Babylon for some time, except for prisoners.

A parallel that supports this interpretation of events occurred in AD 70 when Jerusalem was under siege by the Romans. The general of the army, Titus, gave orders to crucify any Jews who tried to escape the besieged city. For a while over five hundred Jews were nailed to crosses each day just outside the city until the lack of wood for crosses ended the executions.

Far more important than the fugitive's arrival in Babylon were the consequences of his arrival for Ezekiel. As he had promised, the Lord lifted the dumbness that he had imposed on Ezekiel seven and a half years earlier (v. 22; see also 24:27; 3:26-27).

A Rebuke of False Claims of Ownership (33:23-29)

Now that Jerusalem had fallen, it would be reasonable to assume that the attitude of the survivors would change. Surely their pride and rebellious spirit had been broken, and they would turn back to God. Unfortunately, such a change did not take place. They refused to admit that they were being punished for their sins. They argued that Abraham was only one person, yet God had given possession of the land to him. They reasoned that since they possessed the land and there were so many of them, that God's blessings rested on them, as it had on Abraham (v. 24).

Their reasoning seemed logical: (1) "Abraham was godly; (2) he possessed the land; (3) we possess the land; (4) therefore, we are godly—we are Abraham's true heirs!" The flaw in their reasoning was the fourth statement. They possessed the land only because of God's continued mercy. How could they believe they deserved the land? They were still worshiping their idols, eating meat not drained of its blood (v. 25; see Lev. 17:10-14), killing, and committing adultery. Because they refused to repent, God said the desolation of the land was going to continue by sword and pestilence. Then perhaps they would repent and acknowledge that their sins had brought the calamity on the land.

Ezekiel's Acclaim by a Fickle People (33:30-33)

Ezekiel was now a celebrity among the exiles in Babylon. He had been proved to be a true prophet because his judgment messages against Jerusalem had been fulfilled (see Deut. 18:22 for the mark of a true prophet). Further, his recently regained ability to speak had convinced them that he enjoyed a special relationship with God. Wherever they gathered in small groups to talk, Ezekiel was the center of conversation. They flocked to hear what else he might have to say.

The Lord warned Ezekiel not to be deceived by all the attention he was receiving. Although they might throng around him in awed respect and appear to be God's devout, obedient people, they had not changed. They would listen, but they would not obey. With their lips they would express their devotion to the Lord, but in their hearts they were devoted to their own interests. In reality, they were attracted to Ezekiel in the same way they would flock to hear a singer with a beautiful voice. Ezekiel was no more to them than an entertainer!

Wicked Shepherds and a Good Shepherd (34:1-31)

The shepherd was used as a figure for a ruler by many prophets (for example, 1 Kings 22:17; Jer. 10:21; 23:1-4; Mic. 5:5; Zech. 10:2-3; 11:3-8). However, the comparison of a ruler and his subjects to the shepherd with his flock is not limited to the Old Testament. King Hammurabi of Babylon (1728-1686 BC) called himself the "shepherd of men" and the "supplier of pasture and water." Merodach Baladan, ruler of Babylon around 710 BC, compared himself to a shepherd whose duty it is to collect the sheep that are scattered. The Egyptian pharaoh was described in song as the shepherd through whom his subjects lived and breathed.

The shepherd as a figure for the ruler was appropriate because being a shepherd was such a well-known occupation in the ancient Near East and also because his responsibilities paralleled those of a ruler in many respects. It is quite likely that Jesus had Ezekiel 34 in mind when he spoke about the Good Shepherd (John 10:1-18).

Judgment on the Wicked Shepherds (34:1-10)

One of the functions of a shepherd was to provide food, water, and a resting place for the sheep (see Ps. 23:2). The Lord accused Israel's "shepherds" of eating the sheep and clothing themselves with the sheep's wool; that is, the rulers were mercilessly exploiting the common people to enrich themselves (v. 3).

Another function of the shepherd was to care for the sheep's needs. He took care of the sick sheep, dressed their wounds, and hunted for sheep that strayed from the flock. The Lord accused Israel's "shepherds" of negligence in all these responsibilities. Instead of taking care of their people and being concerned about their needs, they used force and harshness in dealing with their people (v. 4).

The third major responsibility of the shepherd was to protect the sheep from danger. He carried a staff that could be used as a weapon against a wild beast that might attack the flock. With its curved end, the staff also could be used to pull a sheep out of a crevice into which it had fallen. Judah's "shepherds" had failed to provide protection for their people. Their policies had brought nothing but disaster and suffering to their subjects. As a result of the failures of Judah's kings, the nation was destroyed, and the people were scattered as captives or fugitives. They were like sheep without a shepherd (vv. 5-6).

The owner of a flock would discharge a shepherd who failed to provide for the sheep's physical needs or who was negligent in protecting the sheep while they were grazing. In the same way, God "discharged" the rulers of Judah because they had failed in their duties to their people. With the fall of Jerusalem, the monarchy came to an end. The rulers could no longer exploit their people and ignore their needs. God himself had rescued his people by allowing Judah to fall to the Babylonians (v. 10).

God as the Good Shepherd (34:11-16)

With the rulers of Judah out of the way, God announced that he was going to take over the duties they had neglected. He would take care of his flock without delegating the authority to someone else. He would do all the things a good shepherd should do—seek out and rescue the scattered sheep (v. 12), feed the sheep (vv. 13-14), give them rest from their enemies (v. 15), and take care of those that were injured (v. 16). Ezekiel is not the only one who described God as a loving shepherd (see also Isa. 40:11; Jer. 31:10; Pss. 23:1; 80:1; 95:7).

There are messianic implications in verses 11-16 that are spelled out even more clearly in verse 23 and in 37:24. In these verses the Lord promised a shepherd as ruler over his people who will be of the family of David (see also Jer. 23:4-6 for a similar messianic statement).

Judgment of the Sheep (34:17-22)

God's judgment was not limited to the rulers, although they bore a major responsibility for the calamity that had befallen Judah. In light of what he had said in chapter 18, we are not surprised that Ezekiel again reminded each individual of his accountability before God. Not only did the leaders exploit and mistreat the people, but the people exploited one another. They were like sheep pushing and shoving for the best grazing spot and for the first drink of water at resting time, leaving muddied, polluted waters for others to drink from. Each one, great or lowly, would be judged on the basis of his treatment of the other "sheep" (vv. 20-22). These verses give assurance that God takes the side of the weak and the downtrodden (see Matt. 5:5; 11:28-30).

A Shepherd from David's Family (34:23-24)

Earlier in chapter 34 God said he was going to assume the role of shepherd of his people (vv. 11-16). Now he announces that this shepherd will be his servant David. When Ezekiel's audiences heard these words, they must have understood them to mean that the throne would be restored to a descendant of David. The Jewish people have never believed that David would actually be raised from the dead to reassume his throne. Instead, they looked for a ruler with David's qualities—a great military and political leader and a man after God's own heart.

Christians see the fulfillment of these words in the kingship of Jesus Christ, whom the New Testament is careful to link by genealogy to David and the tribe of Judah (Matt. 1:2,6,16).

Promise of a Covenant of Peace (34:25-31)

Jeremiah spoke about a New Covenant that God would make with his people (Jer. 31:31-34). Ezekiel describes that New Covenant as a "covenant of peace" (v. 25). It is expressed in terms of physical and political blessing. Wild animals will no longer roam the land, so that a person could even sleep in the woods without fear (v. 25). The rain will fall in its season, thus causing the earth to produce its fruit in abundance. The Old Testament frequently speaks of rain and abundant harvests as God's blessing (see for example, Deut. 28:12; Hos. 2:21-22; Joel 3:18; Amos 9:13-14; Zech. 8:12).

It will be a time when the covenant people will be free from the yoke of any other nation. They will not experience fear, hunger, or the ridicule of other nations. The description of the covenant of peace concludes with the figure found throughout the chapter, that of the shepherd and the sheep. The Lord will be the shepherd, and his people will be his sheep (v. 31).

The "covenant of peace" is also mentioned in Numbers 25:12; Isaiah 54:10; Ezekiel 37:26; and Malachi 2:5. It describes an age of peace when people will live in harmony with God, with themselves, and with one another. The covenant relationship that God offers to every person through Christ brings peace with God, with self, and with others.

Another Message of Judgment Against Edom (35:1-15)

Various explanations have been offered for Ezekiel's second message of judgment against Edom (see 25:12-14 for the first). Some scholars think it is part of the first message that somehow became separated. Some think it reflects the intense hostility between Edom and Israel that goes back to Esau and Jacob (Gen. 27:41). Except in verse 15 (where it is translated as "Idumea" in the KJV), Edom is addressed in these verses as "Mount Seir." Seir was the chief mountain range in Edom located south of the Dead Sea.

God was against Edom and announced that he was going to make her a wasteland. Three sins of Edom are named in these verses as justification for her punishment: (1) her perpetual hatred of Israel and her participation as an ally of Babylon in the destruction of Jerusalem (v. 5); (2) her determination to seize the territory of both Israel and Judah (v. 10); and (3) her arrogance and gloating over the downfall of the house of Israel (vv. 12-15).

The Lord warned that he was going to deal with Edom on the

same basis as she had dealt with Judah (v. 11). It was a frightening threat, as no one should want to be judged on the basis of his treatment of other people. As the Edomites had rejoiced over the destruction of Judah, so other nations would rejoice over Edom's desolation (vv. 14-15).

Restoration of Israel and Its People (36:1-38)

At first glance there seems to be no relationship between chapter 35, which is addressed to Edom, and chapter 36, which is addressed to Israel. However, chapter 35 is actually an introduction to chapter 36. The key to the relationship of the two chapters is found in the word *mountain*. By contrast to judgment pronounced against "Mount Seir" (35:2), the "mountains of Israel" (36:1) are going to be restored.

Passages in the Old Testament that speak of a return of Israel are sometimes severed from their historical context by some interpreters to make them predictive of the establishment of the Jewish nation of Israel in the twentieth century. Whatever else may be implied by Ezekiel's messages of the return of the Israelites to their land, it should be emphasized that he was first of all bringing comfort to people who lived in the sixth century BC. He was assuring *that* generation of God's continuing love for them.

Judgment on Israel's Oppressors (36:1-7)

Before Jerusalem fell, the Lord had instructed Ezekiel to address the "mountains of Israel" (6:2). It was a harsh message of judgment on the people of Judah and their idols. Those who heard the first message may have anticipated another stinging denunciation when Ezekiel again began, "O mountains of Israel" (36:1).

However, this time God's concern was for the mistreatment his people were receiving at the hands of their enemies. It was a complete reversal of the messages to the "mountains" of chapter 6. Those who had gloated over Judah's fall and seized her land for themselves were making her the object of their malicious talk and slander. Their derision brought the Lord to the defense of his people. In his jealous wrath God swore that the nations roundabout who had harmed Judah were themselves going to experience his scorn. A sin against God's people is a sin against God.

Restoration of the Land (36:8-15)

Ancient invaders frequently practiced a "scorched-earth" policy to bring their enemies to submission. Fields and forests were burned to deprive the native population of food and building materials (see Zech. 11:1-3). Nebuchadnezzar's year-and-a-half siege of Jerusalem had been particularly destructive on Judah. The fields lay uncultivated and ravaged. The situation must have looked bleak to the survivors.

They probably found it difficult to believe Ezekiel when he announced that the exiles were soon going to return home (v. 8) and that their native land would once again be tilled and crops harvested. Cities would be rebuilt, and the decimated population would increase. God's future blessings on his people would exceed his former blessings.

The history of Israel and Judah had been filled with sorrow and tragedy. Wicked leaders and idolatrous people had brought sword, disease, and famine to the nation time and time again. In these verses God addressed the land as though it were a person. He told the land it would "no longer bereave them of children" (v. 12); that is, the wars of the past that had caused the deaths of so many innocent children were ending. In addition, the land would not continue to be an object of ridicule by her neighbors.

Explanation of Israel's Punishment (36:16-21)

The Lord explained why the land had suffered such a severe blow. It was because the inhabitants had defiled it by their immoral conduct. He named two of their crimes—idolatry and bloodshed. He could have added oppression, adultery, drunkenness, dishonesty, and other sins. Such sins were to the Lord like the "uncleanness of a woman in her impurity" (v. 17; see Lev. 15:19).

As punishment, he had scattered them among the nations (v. 19). Even their presence as exiles in other lands brought dishonor to the Lord, for people were ridiculing Judah's God. They said he was not powerful enough to protect his people. If he had been, they said the exiles would never have been forced to leave their land.

Judah's enemies shared an ancient belief that a god had power only in the geographical region occupied by the tribe or nation that worshiped him. He was supposed to protect from harm those who believed in him. His failure to do so proved in the popular mind that a god was too weak to protect his people and therefore was not worthy to be worshiped. The other nations failed to understand that it was because of God's concern for the honor of his holy name that he drove his own people out of the land. Not to punish them would have opened him to the charge of being indifferent to sin.

God speaks of his "holy name" four times in this chapter (vv. 20, 21,22,23). Names in the ancient world had a great deal more significance than simply to distinguish one person from another. It was believed that a name revealed something about the nature and attributes of a person (see, for example, Ex. 33:19; 34:6-7; 1 Sam. 25:25). It was also believed that a person became like the name given him; therefore parents chose their children's names carefully. *Joshua, Hosea,* and *Jesus* were popular names in Jewish families because they all come from a word that means "deliver" or "save." Many Jewish parents hoped their sons would grow up to be the deliverer or savior of Israel from nations that oppressed them. When the angel announced the name to be given to the Christ child, he gave it a spiritual rather than political significance: "He will save his people from their sins" (Matt. 1:21).

Not only did God's punishment of his people show that his was a moral rule, but it also revealed his love for them. Genuine love always has the best interest of the beloved at heart. Sometimes that interest is best served by chastisement and correction.

Cleansing and Restoration (36:22-38)

In the preceding verses the Lord explained that he punishes for the sake of his name. Then in verses 22-24 he told the Israelites that he also was going to restore them for the same reason.

He made it quite clear that it was not for anything they had done or deserved but only to bring honor to his name that he was about to act. By his deliverance of them, God would vindicate his name they had profaned by their conduct. By his mighty act of deliverance of his people from their enemies, God would vindicate his holiness, and the pagan nations would have to acknowledge his existence and power.

Israel's uncleanness would be removed when God sprinkled clean water on them (v. 25). Water was used by the priests for ritual washings to remove ceremonial defilement that resulted from breaking God's laws (see Ex. 30:17-21; Lev. 14:52; Num. 19:17-19). An Israelite who was "unclean" according to the law could not participate in the worship of God through the ceremonies at the Temple. The application of water on him symbolized that his sins had been forgiven because they had been dealt with in the manner prescribed by the law. The Lord promised that Israel would be cleansed of all her sins, including her idolatry.

In times past the Lord had frequently spoken of the hardness of heart of his people (for example, Deut. 15:7; 1 Sam. 6:6; Ps. 95:8). Now, in one of the most significant statements in the entire Book of Ezekiel, the prophet takes up a theme previously mentioned in 11:19-21 and 18:30-32. Once again the Lord announced that he was going to give his people a new heart and a new spirit (v. 26; compare Acts 2:4). He was going to remove their heart of stone and give them a heart of flesh; that is, their stubborn defiance of God would be replaced by loving, sensitive obedience.

With God's Spirit dwelling in them, they would obey him not out of a sense of duty, compulsion, or threat, but because they wanted to (see 2 Cor. 5:14 for the New Testament motivation for obeying God). The entire passage is a remarkable anticipation of the New Covenant that was established by Jesus Christ, a covenant characterized by regeneration and the indwelling of the Spirit.

Verses 25-32 describe the qualities of a person who has received a "new heart." He is forgiven and cleansed from sin (v. 25), endowed with a new nature (v. 26), obedient (v. 27), and secure ("you shall dwell in the land," v. 28). In addition, he is blessed (vv. 29-30). In the Old Testament, blessing is frequently expressed in terms of material prosperity, such as an abundant food supply and fruitfulness of the trees and fields (see Amos 9:13; Zech. 8:12).

Another quality of the person with a "new heart" is a changed attitude toward sin (v. 31). God's forgiveness should never instill a spirit of pride in any person. God told his people that it was not for their sake that he acted (v. 32). There was nothing inherently good about them, and there was nothing they had done that would bring about their cleansing. The new heart and the new spirit were gifts of God through his grace (see Rom. 6:23; 11:6; Eph. 2:8-9).

The restoration of the land is closely linked to God's forgiveness of his people in verses 33-36. When their sins are cleansed, God will rebuild their ruined cities and people will once again live in them (v. 33). The neglected land will again be cultivated (v. 34). Visitors from other nations will be amazed by the fruitfulness of the land, comparing it to Eden (v. 35). They will acknowledge that only the Lord could have transformed such a ruined and desolate land (v. 36).

God does not impose his will or his blessings on anyone. Lest the people who heard Ezekiel's words misinterpret them, the closing verses of the chapter reaffirm the principle of freedom of choice (vv. 37-38). He told the Israelites they would have to ask for God's blessings. The crowning blessing the Lord promised to give them was an abundance of children (see Ps. 127:5). In these verses the increase in population is compared to the great flocks of animals that were taken to Jerusalem for sacrifice during the times of the appointed feasts. When the desolate cities are once again filled with people, then the house of Israel will know that the Lord is what he claims to be.

Vision of the Valley of Dry Bones (37:1-14)

Judah as a nation was dead. The city of Jerusalem with its Temple had been destroyed. The people who survived were paralyzed by a feeling of hopelessness. Ezekiel continued to combat the despair that had engulfed them. One of his best-known messages of encouragement is found in chapter 37. It came to Ezekiel as another of his visions from the Lord.

The Vision (37:1-10)

Each of Ezekiel's visions is introduced by an unusual phrase, "the hand of the Lord was upon" him (1:3; 8:1; 37:1; 40:1). It suggests some kind of ecstatic experience through which the prophet had an unusual awareness of God's presence. It also suggests a gripping compulsion to do God's will. The vision of the valley of dry bones must have occurred soon after the fall of Jerusalem because the people were in a mood of total despair. They were saying, "Our hope is lost; we are clean cut off" (v. 11).

Even as Ezekiel had experienced movement from one place to another in previous visions (3:12,14; 8:3; 11:24), he was now transported by the Spirit of the Lord to a valley that was full of bones (v. 1). No attempt should be made to identify the actual location of the valley, as there was no real valley filled with bones. The experience was visionary and symbolic.

Bone is from a word that means "to be powerful" and reflects an ancient belief that the bones of the body were associated with health and strength. The extreme dryness of the bones emphasized Judah's utter hopelessness (v. 2).

The Lord asked Ezekiel if he believed the bones could once again become living persons (v. 3). It would have been presumptuous for the prophet to answer yes, as he did not know God's intentions. On the other hand, if he responded no, he would have revealed unbelief about God's power. Therefore, the safest answer he could give was, "O Lord God, thou knowest" (v. 3)! A faith response can accept the possibility of resurrection in the face of the hopelessness of death (John 11:25).

The answer apparently satisfied the Lord, for he continued by telling Ezekiel to speak to the bones. He instructed him to inform the bones that the Lord would put breath in them and restore their flesh. As a result of their resurrection, the bones would know that the one who made them live was the Lord. Notice that the verses emphasize the word of the Lord as the source of the resurrection of the bones.

Ezekiel could have objected that it would be futile to preach to dry bones, but he did not. Though it appeared foolish for Ezekiel to preach to dead bones, it reminds us that people are saved by the foolishness of preaching (1 Cor. 1:21). Ezekiel proclaimed the word. There was a rattling noise, the result of bone joining bone. The word *rattling* has also been translated to mean an earthquake occurred when the bones came together (v. 7).

Ezekiel watched as flesh and skin formed on the bones, but the bodies were still lifeless because there was no breath in them. The same Hebrew word, *ruach,* can mean "breath" or "spirit," but in verse 5 most translations understand *ruach* to mean "breath."

The Lord told Ezekiel to command the breath from the four winds (that is, from the four corners of the earth) to enter the lifeless bodies (v. 9). He did as commanded and watched as a great throng of bodies came to life and stood up. The preacher who proclaims the Word to people who are dead in their sins and sees them experience new life feels the same excitement Ezekiel must have felt when he saw the dead bones come to life.

Interpretation of the Vision (37:11-14)

Lest there be any misunderstanding about the meaning of the vision, the Lord interpreted it for Ezekiel. The bones represented all the people of Israel. As a nation they were dead, but God said he was going to put new life in them, that is, he was going to restore the nation and bring back the people from Exile.

The meaning of this vision is clear and has not been disputed. It describes a nation that is dead but will be revived. However, the principal question raised in connection with the vision is whether it assumed an existing belief in bodily resurrection. Notice verse 12: "I will open your graves, and raise you from your graves"; this seems to imply knowledge of bodily resurrection.

Many scholars say the Hebrews did not develop a belief in bodily resurrection until shortly before the Christian era. They insist that in 37:1-14 there is no evidence that Ezekiel either believed in or revealed any knowledge of a doctrine of the resurrection of the dead. It is true that the Old Testament is not very specific about belief in life after death. Isaiah 26:19 and Dan. 12:2 are the clearest indisputable expressions of resurrection. However, unless the people already believed in resurrection, the analogy would have been foolish to them. Effective teachers work from the known to the unknown.

If resurrection had been a questionable or unknown idea to the Israelites of Ezekiel's day, the vision would have communicated the opposite to them from what was intended. Instead of saying that the resurrection of Israel as a nation was as certain as bodily resurrection, it would have been like saying, "Israel's restoration is as certain as man's ability to fly without any mechanical aids."

Two Sticks Become One (37:15-28)

All of chapter 37 has as its theme the restoration of the house of Israel (a term that includes all twelve tribes). The first fourteen verses express that theme through a vision; the remaining verses express it by means of a symbolic act.

As in earlier symbolic acts (see introduction to ch. 4), the Lord instructed Ezekiel to perform a symbolic act and then to explain its meaning. He told Ezekiel to take a stick and write the word *Judah* on it (representing the Southern Kingdom that ended in 587 BC). On a second stick he was to write *Joseph* (represented by his son Ephraim as one of the tribes in the Northern Kingdom that ended in 722 BC). Then he was to join the sticks and grasp the joined ends in his fist to give the appearance that the two had become one stick.

Some interpreters insist that a miracle took place, and the dead pieces of wood were actually fused into one unbroken stick. We should never place restrictions on what God can do, but miracles were not characteristic of the symbolic acts of the prophets. There has been nothing miraculous about any of Ezekiel's symbolic acts up to this point. If miracles had been characteristic of the symbolic acts, the audiences would have been so intrigued by the miracles that they might have paid no attention to the messages the acts were intended to convey.

The joined sticks symbolized the reuniting of the kingdoms of Israel and Judah that had separated at the time of Solomon's death in 922 BC (1 Kings 12:1-20). God was going to bring the people of both nations back from the lands where they had been scattered and establish them as one nation under one king (v. 22). They would no longer defile themselves by idolatry and other sins but would be a cleansed people whom God could claim as "my people" (v. 23).

Once again the Lord renewed his promise of a Davidic king for the united people (see 34:23-24 for comments on David as king). An idyllic description of the messianic kingdom follows that repeats many ideas Ezekiel has expressed earlier.

Ruled by one shepherd (see 34:23), the people will carefully observe God's laws (v. 24). They will dwell in the land forever that was given to their ancestor Jacob centuries earlier (see 20:5-6). God will make an everlasting covenant of peace with them (see 34:25) and multiply them (see 36:37).

God's sanctuary will be set in their midst as a symbol of his dwelling presence among his people and will never again be removed from their midst. The "sanctuary" of verse 26 is interpreted two ways: (1) literally, as a rebuilt Temple in Jerusalem and (2) symbolically, as another way of referring to God's presence with his people (see Rev. 21:22). When God restores and exalts his people, then other nations will know that it was the Lord who set Israel apart (v. 28).

God's Judgment on Gog (38:1 to 39:29)

Chapters 38—39 are among the most difficult in the Book of Ezekiel to interpret. There is general agreement that they constitute a unity, but beyond that, interpretations of the two chapters vary widely. The narrative itself is not difficult to understand. It describes an invader called "Gog, of the land of Magog." This invader attacks the defenseless Israelites, who have returned to their land and are in the process of rebuilding. The attack arouses the anger of God, who comes to the rescue of his people and annihilates the enemy.

The interpretation of these two chapters hinges on how "Gog, of the land of Magog" is identified. Is Gog to be understood literally as an actual nation, and if so, what is the nation? Interpreting it as a literal nation, some Bible students insist that chapters 38—39 describe a future gathering of world powers against Israel under the leadership of Russia, resulting in the battle of Armageddon.

On the other hand, many scholars do not take chapters 38—39 as a literal description of something that is going to happen sometime in the future. They understand the language as an apocalyptic literary form and therefore interpret it symbolically. Thus, the main thrust of the message is that Gog symbolizes the forces of evil who are determined to destroy the people of God. In the end, however, God will be victorious over all evil. These interpreters insist that a more specific interpretation that names nations and sets dates depends on speculation and the ingenuity of the interpreter rather than on sound exegesis.

The apocalyptic literary form, found also in the Books of Daniel and Revelation, is characterized by the use of symbolic language (for example, the use of animals and numbers as symbols of something else). It assumes that the symbols can be interpreted by those who understand such things. Apocalyptic writing also focuses on events in the last times and on judgment and a new age to come. It frequently emphasizes the struggle between the forces of good and evil and is characterized by dramatic elements such as visions, angels, and demonic beings.

A word of caution should be heeded by anyone who attempts to interpret apocalyptic writings, such as are found in Ezekiel 38—39. The caution is to remember that belief in the Bible and interpretations of the Bible are not necessarily the same thing. Someone may disagree with your interpretation, but that does not mean that he rejects belief in the Bible. The Bible student who questions the correctness of interpreting Meshech (38:2) as Moscow or Gomer (38:6) as Germany (as some Bible students do) is not denying the Scriptures, but an interpretation of them. We must always be careful to understand there is a distinction between believing the Bible and believing a particular interpretation of it.

Gog's Military Campaign Against Israel (38:1-16)

It is generally recognized that there are seven distinct messages in Ezekiel 38—39. They are 38:3-9,10-13,14-16,17-23; 39:1-16,17-24, 25-29. Each one begins with "Thus says the Lord God." In an introduction to these messages, Ezekiel is instructed to announce judgment on "Gog, of the land of Magog" (v. 2).

Numerous identifications of "Gog, of the land of Magog" have been proposed by Bible students. They include Babylon; Gyges, king of Lydia (called Gugu in Assyrian records); Gagaia, a barbarian land; a Canaanite deity called Gaga; Alexander the Great; and Antiochus Eupator. The name "Magog" sheds no light on the identity of Gog. It is found in Genesis 10:2 and 1 Chronicles 1:5 in reference to a son of Japheth and a grandson of Noah but is not found in any other ancient documents. Revelation 20:8 changes "Gog, of . . . Magog" to "Gog *and* Magog" and identifies them as "the nations which are at the four corners of the earth."

Whatever his particular identity, Gog is the evil leader of the peoples who make a united assault against the people of God.

Associated with Gog are Meshech and Tubal, mentioned in Genesis 10:2 as sons of Japheth and also mentioned in other ancient documents. Other allies of Gog named are Persia to the east, Cush (another name for Ethiopia), Put (generally considered to be located in Africa, perhaps a part of Libya), Gomer (originally a people from north of the Black Sea), and Beth-togarmah (probably another name for Armenia). Altogether, they represent a coalition of forces from north, east, and southwest of Israel (vv. 5-6).

The Lord warned that he was against all those peoples and will turn them around and put hooks in their jaws and lead them away like captured animals (vv. 3-4; see also 2 Kings 19:28; Isa. 37:29; Ezek. 29:4; Amos 4:2 for a similar figure).

A time will come when these people will gather to attack the Israelites whom the Lord has brought back from the many nations where they had been scattered. They will be dwelling securely once again in their land, unaware that an enemy has gathered and is advancing on them like a great storm cloud that covers the land (v. 9).

This great horde will deliberately set out to attack the people of Israel who are totally unsuspecting and without any means of defense. They will be living in towns without walls or gates that could be barred to protect them from enemies. The enemy anticipates an easy victory and a great amount of plunder. In verse 12 Israel is described as living at "the center of the earth" (literally, "the navel of the earth"). The unusual expression suggests the importance of these people to God.

Merchants of Sheba, Dedan, and Tarshish will watch with anticipation as the enemy horde prepares to attack (v. 13). They already envision the profit from the plunder that will be brought to them for trade.

In verses 14-16 we are told that it is God who will bring this great army on horseback against his people. There is no inconsistency between these verses and verse 10, which seems to say they devised the evil scheme themselves. God has sovereign control over all events and will allow the enemy to attack; but in the end his purposes, not theirs, will be accomplished. Through God's victory over them, other nations will know him when his holiness is vindicated before their eyes (v. 16). Gog is not a helpless pawn brought to ruin by an all-powerful but insensitive God. Gog will choose of his own free will to attack God's people, but the Lord will turn his evil plans into a victory for himself (see Rom 8:28).

The Destruction of Gog's Army (38:17-23)

Apparently the invasion of Judah by Gog had been predicted by prophets of the Lord "in former days" (v. 17). It is impossible to know which prophets are intended, although Numbers 24:17-24; Deuteronomy 32:43; Psalm 9:15; Joel 3:1-16; Jeremiah 4:5-31; Daniel 2:44-45; Zephaniah 1:14-18; 3:8 have been suggested. Prophets who spoke of an enemy "from the north" may have been intended (Isa. 14:31; 41:25; Jer. 1:14-15; 4:6; Zeph. 2:13). Gog has been equated with Assyria, described as an invader in Isaiah 10:5-16 and Micah 5:5, but this is unlikely. One possible explanation is that the prophecy referred to by Ezekiel is not preserved in the Old Testament. Not every word of the Lord to a prophet has been included in the Bible.

The consequence of Gog's invasion of the land of Israel will be to arouse the wrath of the Lord against Gog (v. 18). There will be an earthquake of immense proportions that will be felt by mankind and beasts alike. Mountains will crumble, and city walls will collapse (compare Hag. 2:21-22). Such panic and confusion will be created among the demoralized enemy that they will turn on each other with the sword. All nature will join in the attack against Gog, including torrential rains, hail, fire, and brimstone (v. 22). A multitude of nations will recognize that the greatness and holiness of God are responsible for the destruction of the enemy horde.

Chapter 39 will describe in greater detail the visitation of God's wrath on Gog and her allies.

A "Mopping Up" Task (39:1-16)

The sovereign God is against Gog and therefore will deliberately entice him to attack Israel (vv. 1-2). When the attack comes, God will fight for his people. He will make Gog's weapons useless, and the enemy horde will be destroyed on the hillsides and open fields of Israel. Their unburied corpses will be devoured by birds of prey and wild animals (a "feast" to be described in greater detail in verses 17-20). Judgment will not be limited to the attacking enemy but will include allies and sympathizers in distant parts of the earth.

The conquest of Judah in 587 BC and the consequent dispersion of her people caused other nations to doubt God's power and majesty. Therefore, the purpose of his intervention will be to bring an end to the ridicule and blasphemy against his holy name by those who have oppressed his people. Those nations that formerly scoffed at God as being powerless will be forced to acknowledge that he is the Lord when they see the destruction of Israel's enemies.

The "mopping up" operation described in verses 9-20 is intended to show just how vast are the multitudes that will assemble against defenseless Israel and how great their slaughter will be. It will require seven years for the Israelites to burn and destroy all the weapons of the enemy (v. 9). The wood used to make the shields, bows and arrows, war clubs, and spears will be so abundant that the people will not have to cut down trees to provide fuel. The plunder taken from the destroyed enemy will be recompense for the plunder they had taken from the Israelites.

The Lord will designate a place for the burial of the enemy (v. 11). Its location has been translated as "the valley of the passengers" (KJV), "the valley of those who pass by" (NASB), "Valley of the Travelers" (RSV) and "Valley of Abarim" (NEB). Located east of the

Dead Sea, it will be renamed the Valley of Hamon-gog (that is, the multitude of Gog).

Mosaic law required that corpses be buried in order to cleanse the land from pollution (Lev. 5:2; Num. 5:2; 19:16; 35:33-34). By burying them outside the borders of Israel, cleansing would be assured. It will require seven months to bury the horde of Gog's armies and thus cleanse the land (v. 12). All Israel will participate in the burial of the enemy. The valley will be so clogged with corpses that travelers will not be able to pass through it.

At the end of the seven months, men will be appointed to go through the land searching for any corpses that might have been overlooked. Their task will be to make sure that no source of pollution remains in the land. When they find the bones of an enemy soldier, they will place a marker beside the bones. Other men will come behind them and take the bones to the Valley of Hamon-gog for burial. The land will not be considered clean again until all the corpses have been removed.

A Feast for Birds and Animals (39:17-24)

The Lord told Ezekiel to announce a sacrificial feast for the birds and wild animals. A similar description of this feast is found in Revelation 19:17-18. A sacrificial feast for the Lord is mentioned in Isaiah 34:6; Jeremiah 46:10, and Zephaniah 1:7-9 and probably serves as the basis for the feast described here.

Instead of the usual rams, lambs, goats, and bulls that were ordinarily offered as sacrifices, here the sacrificial victims will be the princes and mighty men who have attacked God's people. The birds and animals will feed on the flesh of these men and drink their blood. The victims are compared to the choicest fatlings of Bashan that were preferred for sacrifices by the Jewish people (v. 18). The birds and wild animals that are attracted to the carnage of the battlefield will fill themselves until they can eat no more.

The description of the feast in verses 17-20 is grisly and repulses the reader, but its purpose is to impress on all people the horror of coming under the judgment of God. Today there is a tendency in the pulpit not to dwell on the horrors of God's judgment, with the result that many people have lost all fear of that judgment.

As a consequence of the annihilation of Gog and his allies, all nations will know that they have witnessed God's judgment. Even the Israelites, who had a history of faithlessness and idolatry, will know from that day forward that the Lord is their God (v. 22). Other nations will understand that Israel's years of captivity were God's judgment on his people. He hid his face from them for a time because of their sins that had contaminated them (v. 23).

A New Beginning for Jacob (39:25-29)

Jacob was the father of twelve sons who became the ancestors of the Israelite tribes. His name was changed to Israel after his encounter with God at Peniel (Gen. 32:28), so his descendants are often called Israelites (literally, "sons of Israel") in the Old Testament. However, as in verse 25, they are also sometimes referred to in the Bible as Jacob (for example, Isa. 41:8,21; 48:20; Luke 1:33; Rom. 11:26).

With the end of Israel's punishment (already anticipated in verses 21-24) and the judgment of her enemies completed, the Lord announced that he was about to "restore the fortunes" of his people (v. 25; "I will bring again the captivity," KJV). This expression is used frequently in the Old Testament to describe the restoration of God's blessings on a nation or a person (for example, 16:53; 29:14; Ps. 14:7; Amos 9:14).

The Lord will act to restore his people out of concern for his holy name. If he allows his people to remain defeated and scattered, other nations will not believe that he is the all-powerful God. Therefore, he will vindicate his holiness before the other nations by restoring his people to their land. The descendants of Jacob will put their shame and treachery behind them and will acknowledge the Lord as their God when they once again dwell securely in their land. God's restored favor will enable them to erase the memory of their long history of faithlessness.

The Lord will no longer hide his face from his people in disapproval. Instead, he "will pour" out his Spirit on the people of Israel (v. 29; see also 36:25-31 and Joel 2:28 for a similar promise). The Hebrew of this verse actually says "I have poured out my Spirit," even though Israel has not yet experienced that blessing. This is an example of what is called in the Hebrew language the prophetic perfect tense, a construction that speaks with certainty of something that is going to happen as though it has already happened. It was as good as done because God said the Spirit was going to be poured out on his people.

Vision of a Restored and Exalted People of God
40:1 to 48:35

No part of the Book of Ezekiel is more important than chapters 40—48. Though at first glance these chapters do not appear to be related to what has preceded, they, in fact, are the climax of the book. They describe a time when the people of Israel will finally attain what God promised to Abraham centuries before; that is, they will be blessed and they will be a blessing (Gen. 12:1-3). They will live at peace in the land that God set aside as their possession. Most important of all, they will acknowledge the Lord as their God and worship him only. Jerusalem will be renamed "The Lord is there" in recognition of the Lord's abiding presence in the midst of his people (48:35).

When we remember what the Jewish people were experiencing when Ezekiel spoke these words, we can appreciate more fully the impact the message must have had on the people in exile. Judah was no longer a nation. Jerusalem and the Temple had been destroyed, and many of her people had been taken captive or had fled to other countries. At a time when it seemed there was no hope, Ezekiel announced a glorious future for the people of God.

God's revelation to Ezekiel concerning the future of the people came as a vision to the prophet. It is appropriate that the book begins with a vision and ends with a vision. Ezekiel's closing vision is the longest recorded vision in the entire Old Testament. Bible students are in complete agreement that the intent of these chapters was to restore hope in the hearts of a discouraged and defeated people. However, there is no other part of the Book of Ezekiel about which there is so much controversy as to its meaning, with the possible exception of chapters 38—39!

There are at least four ways that these chapters have been interpreted. The first could be called a historical interpretation. Those who follow this approach believe that Ezekiel was giving a blueprint for a Temple he expected to be built when the exiles returned from their Babylonian Exile. This Temple would have been even larger than Solomon's magnificent Temple. However, neither

Haggai nor Zechariah mention Ezekiel's Temple plan, and both of them were involved in the reconstruction of the Temple that began in 520 BC. Their Temple did not follow the grandiose proportions of Ezekiel's Temple. In fact, those still living who remembered Solomon's Temple ridiculed the new Temple and said it was nothing like the previous structure (Hag. 2:3). Ezekiel's Temple plan was much too elaborate to have been compared unfavorably with Solomon's Temple. Also to call it a "blueprint" overlooks the fact that the description is not sufficiently detailed for a builder to follow, since no heights are given, only floor dimensions.

Another argument against interpreting Ezekiel's Temple as the one that was rebuilt under the leadership of Haggai and Zechariah is the description of a river that flowed from the new Temple (47:1-12). The river described by Ezekiel transcends historical reality.

A second way of interpreting these chapters is to regard them as allegorical. Allegory is the use of a figurative story to present a meaning which is implied but not directly stated. The allegorical method of interpretation was quite popular in the early centuries of the Christian church and resulted in all kinds of fanciful and farfetched interpretations. One allegorical interpretation of Ezekiel 40—48 understands the rebuilt Temple as symbolizing the establishment of the Christian church. Another allegorical interpretation is that it symbolizes the redeemed of all the ages worshiping God in heaven. Yet another allegorical interpretation says the rebuilt Temple is intended to symbolize the characteristics of the redeemed people of God (such as holiness, consecration, unity). There is no limit to biblical interpretations that can be derived allegorically, and who can say which is valid?

A third way of interpreting Ezekiel 40—48 is called the dispensational or futuristic approach. Those of this persuasion believe the Temple described by Ezekiel will be rebuilt just before the millennium, and the sacrificial system will be restored by the Jewish people. This interpretation causes difficulty for many Bible students, as it appears to suggest that Christ's sacrifice on the cross was not God's final and climactic redemptive work. Instead, in this scheme the goal of his redemptive plan is the restoration of animal sacrifice.

A fourth way of interpreting these chapters is to recognize that they employ the apocalyptic literary form (see the introduction to chapter 38 for an explanation of this form). Thus, the intent of the vision is to describe God's kingdom in understandable terms. The vision tells us symbolically that (1) God has already devised a redemptive plan for his people that is perfect in every detail; (2) God will abide forever in the midst of his people; (3) worship of God will be central and all-important to the redeemed community; and (4) God's blessings will flow to every part of the world. Expressed another way, the vision symbolizes everything that God is and that he will do for his people in the coming age.

It is unlikely there will ever be agreement among Bible students as to the exact meaning of Ezekiel's Temple vision. However, it may be some comfort to know that ancient Jewish rabbis also struggled to understand the vision, but without success. They finally said that when Elijah returns, he will answer all the questions about the vision!

A word of caution that was given with chapters 38—39 needs to be repeated with chapters 40—48. If someone differs with your interpretation of these chapters, it does not necessarily mean that he does not believe the Bible. It only means that he is unable to accept your interpretation of it. There is a difference between believing the Bible and believing someone's interpretation of it.

In the controversy over the interpretation of the details of Ezekiel's vision, the purpose of the vision is frequently overlooked. That purpose is stated in 43:10: "that they may be ashamed of their iniquities." The purpose of the vision, then, was to bring the Israelites back to God in Ezekiel's time by revealing his great love and grace that they did not deserve.

A New Temple for Jerusalem (40:1 to 43:27)

The one event that must have shattered the people of Judah more than anything else was the destruction of the Temple by Nebuchadnezzar's armies in 587 BC. They had associated the Temple with the presence of their invincible God and could not believe that he would allow it to be destroyed. At first, many of them must have concluded that their God was not all-powerful, as they had formerly believed. They interpreted the destruction of the Temple as his defeat.

Later, however, while in exile they began to remember the warnings of prophets such as Micah and Jeremiah (Mic. 3:12; Jer. 7:14-15; 26:6), who told them that Jerusalem would be destroyed as punishment for their sins. This realization led to another disturbing question: If God had not been defeated, had he cast off his people forever? The announcement of a new Temple was the answer.

The Vision Begins (40:1-4)

Ezekiel's final vision occurred in the twenty-fifth year of his exile in Babylon and fourteen years after Jerusalem's conquest (v. 1). That would have been 573 BC. Also, it was the tenth day of the first month. The date may have some intentional association with the Passover season, which began on the fourteenth day of the first month (see Ex. 12:3,6; Lev. 23:5).

As in his previous visions, Ezekiel felt the hand of the Lord on him as he was transported to a high mountain somewhere in Israel (compare 1:3; 3:14; 8:1; 37:1). He noticed a structure on the mountain that appeared to be a city (v. 2) but which is identified in verse 5 as the new Temple. The whole experience was obviously visionary, as the Temple he saw had not actually been built.

Ezekiel noticed a man standing in the gateway of the wall around the Temple. His appearance was like bronze, and he held a measuring stick in his hand, such as builders used. He spoke to Ezekiel and instructed him to pay careful attention to what he was about to see and then to tell the Israelites all he had seen.

The Courts of the Temple (40:5-49)

It will be helpful to the reader in studying the description of the Temple that was shown to Ezekiel to have available a sketch of the Temple. These can be found in Bible encyclopedias or commentaries. Otherwise, one quickly gets lost in the visual details of the Temple as it is described in the following chapters.

The outer court and its gateways (40:5-27).—As the cubit measurement was not uniform in the ancient Near East, the exact length of the measuring stick of six cubits carried by the man is uncertain. A cubit varied between seventeen and twenty-one inches; therefore the measuring stick was somewhere between nine and ten feet long.

The first thing the man did was to measure the wall around the outside of the Temple area. The thickness and the height of the wall were the same as the man's measuring stick—one reed (that is, nine to ten feet in thickness and in height).

Then he walked up the seven steps (see v. 22) leading into the gateway on the east side and measured the threshold of the gate, which was also one reed deep (v. 6). The mention of steps tells us that the entire Temple complex was on a platform that elevated it above the ground surrounding it.

Within the gateway were side rooms which the man also measured (v. 7). There were three rooms on either side of the gateway. They were probably used as guard rooms where Temple officials were stationed to preserve order and to control the crowds who came to the Temple during the festivals. The man also measured the threshold at the inner end of the gateway that adjoined the vestibule. Then he measured the vestibule, or porch, which opened onto the outer court of the Temple (vv. 8,14). The total distance from the front of the gateway to the other end of the inner vestibule was fifty cubits (v. 15). Both the gateway and the vestibule had windows to provide light (v. 16).

The man then escorted Ezekiel through the vestibule into the outer court where the prophet could see rooms around the court, thirty of them altogether (v. 17). The court itself was probably paved with stones. On the far side of the outer court Ezekiel, looking toward the west, could see the gateway leading into the inner court. The distance from where he stood at the edge of the outer court across the pavement to the gateway to the inner court was one hundred cubits (v. 19).

The man escorted Ezekiel to the north side of the outer court where there was a gateway with rooms; it was just like the entrance on the east side. Its dimensions also were the same (vv. 20-22). Standing at the gateway on the north side, Ezekiel could look southward across the pavement of the outer court and see a gateway leading to the inner court just like the gateway on the east side that led to the inner court. The distance across the pavement of the outer court to the entrance to the inner court was the same as on the east side, one hundred cubits (v. 23).

Then the man led Ezekiel around to the south side of the outer court where there was another gateway with rooms, just like the gateways on the east and north sides. Its dimensions were the same as the other gateways (vv. 24-26). Standing at the gateway on the south side, Ezekiel could look northward across the pavement of the outer court and see a gateway leading to the inner court. It was exactly like the gateways on the east and north sides that led into the inner court. The distance across the pavement to the inner court gateway was the same as the distances on the east and north sides, one hundred cubits (v. 27).

The inner court and its gateways (40:28-47).—Next, the man brought Ezekiel to the south gateway that led into the inner court. This gateway to the inner court was constructed just like the outer gateways, with side rooms, windows, and a vestibule, or porch. It was necessary to climb eight steps to enter the gateway that led into the inner court (v. 31), which was on a platform elevated above the platform of the outer court (vv. 28-31).

Then the man brought Ezekiel to the east gateway that led into the inner court from that side (v. 32). This gateway also was constructed just like the other gateways, with side rooms, windows, and a vestibule. Eight steps led up to the gateway that led into the inner court from this side also (vv. 32-34).

Then the man took Ezekiel to the north gateway that led to the inner court from that side. As the reader would expect by now, it was identical with the other gateways (vv. 35-37). The whole Temple structure reveals a careful symmetry in its design.

It should be noted that there was no outside gateway on the west side of the Temple leading into the outer court. Nor was there a gateway on that side leading into the inner court. The outer and inner courts could only be entered from the east, south, and north. This departure from the symmetrical construction on the other three sides was deliberately done to avoid entering the Temple from the rear. Since the Temple faced east, to enter from the west, or back side, would have suggested disrespect for the God whose presence dwelled in the Temple.

There was a room in the vestibule of the inner gate where the burnt offerings were to be washed in preparation for sacrifice. There were two tables on either side in the vestibule of the gateway, on which the burnt, sin, and guilt offerings were slaughtered (vv. 38-41). The same number of tables were also on the outside of the vestibule. The text does not say whether the vestibule on the east, south, or north is being described in these verses. Some believe that the east gateway is intended, but it is possible that each gateway had the same furnishing for receiving the sacrificial animals.

In addition to the tables just described, there were four tables of hewn stone to be used for the burnt offerings. On them were kept the instruments for slaughtering the animals that were selected for the burnt offerings (v. 42). The Septuagint adds that roofs were over the tables to offer protection from rain and heat.

After Ezekiel had carefully observed the gateways and the outer court, the man led him into the inner court. Only priests were allowed to enter the inner court, but Ezekiel was a priest.

In the inner court Ezekiel saw two chambers that were used by the priests. One chamber, facing south, was beside the north gateway and was for the use of the priests who had daily responsibilities in the Temple (v. 45). The other chamber, facing north, was located beside the south gateway and was for the use of the priests in charge of the altar. Only Zadokite priests (descendants of Zadok) could minister before the Lord at the altar. Other Levitical priests could not participate in this sacred function (v. 46; compare Num. 3:6-10; 8:19; 18:1-7).

The inner court was exactly one hundred cubits square. In its center and directly in front of the Temple building was the altar of burnt offering (v. 47; see also Ex. 27:1-8).

The vestibule of the Temple (40:48-49).—After measuring the inner court, the man escorted Ezekiel up a flight of stairs (the Septuagint says there were ten steps) to the vestibule, or porch, of the Temple. There he measured the vestibule. The mention of steps reminds us that the Temple was constructed on a platform that elevated it above the inner court. Altogether there were three series of steps in the Temple complex. The first was from the ground level to the outer court; the second led from the outer court to the inner court; the third series of steps led from the inner court to the Temple vestibule.

Ezekiel noticed pillars on either side of the entrance to the vestibule. They probably corresponded to the pillars called Jachin and Boaz that were in front of Solomon's Temple (v. 49; see 1 Kings 7:21).

The Temple and Its Side Chambers (41:1-26)

Ezekiel's Temple followed a plan that was characteristic of temples in the ancient Near East. It was composed of three principal sections: (1) a vestibule, or entrance porch; (2) a large room, called the nave or holy place; and (3) a smaller room, called the most holy place or holy of holies. The Hebrew people called the three parts (1) the *ulam*, (2) the *hekal*, and (3) the *debir.* Certain sacred articles were kept in the nave, such as the table for the bread of the Presence ("table of shewbread," Num. 4:7, KJV), the altar of incense, and the gold lampstand. The priests were assigned duties for the care of all these articles. The most holy place contained the ark of the covenant and could only be entered by the high priest once a year on the Day of Atonement (see Lev. 16:2,29-30; Heb. 9:7).

The holy place and the most holy place (41:1-4).—The man measured the holy place, or nave, and found it to be forty cubits long and twenty cubits wide (v. 2). He entered the most holy place (without Ezekiel) and took its measurements. It was a square, twenty by twenty cubits (v. 4).

The side chambers (41:5-11).—The walls of the Temple measured by the man were six cubits thick. He also measured the side rooms, which were arranged in three stories, one over the other, with thirty rooms in each story (v. 6). These side chambers were probably store rooms for Temple equipment and furnishings and also for the tithes and offerings the people brought to the Temple.

The building west of the Temple (41:12).—Behind the Temple on the west side of the inner court was a large building seventy cubits wide and ninety cubits long. Its walls were five cubits thick. Its function is not explained, but it was probably some kind of storage area.

Measurements of the Temple area (41:13-15a).—The man measured the outer dimensions of the Temple, the yard, and the building on the west side. The Temple was one hundred cubits long.

Interior decorations of the Temple (41:15b-26).—The interior walls of the Temple were paneled with wood from the floor up to the windows. The likenesses of cherubim and palm trees were carved alternately on the walls. The cherubim, unlike the four-faced cherubim encountered by Ezekiel earlier, had two faces (v. 18; see 1:10). One was the face of a man, and the other was the face of a young lion (v. 19).

Ezekiel saw something that resembled an altar made of wood (v. 22). The man with him called it "the table which is before the Lord." It was probably the table of the bread of the Presence ("table of shewbread," Num. 4:7, KJV).

Double wood doors led from the vestibule of the Temple to the nave and from the nave to the most holy place. They also were carved with cherubim and palm trees. A wooden screen was placed in front of the vestibule on the outside.

The Priests' Chambers (42:1-14)

Chambers to the north of the Temple yard (42:1-10a).—The man then led Ezekiel from the Temple back into the inner court to its north side. There Ezekiel observed a building one hundred cubits long and fifty cubits wide. It was composed of three stories. This structure is not the same as the side chambers described in 41:5-11. The description is somewhat obscure, and it is difficult to visualize the exact appearance and arrangement of the building.

Chambers to the south of the Temple yard (42:10b-12).—An identical building was located in the inner court on the south side.

Purpose of the chambers (42:13-14).—The chambers described in verses 1-12 were set aside as a place for the priests to eat the holy offerings that were brought to them (v. 13; see Num. 18:8-10). The rooms were also used as a place where the priests could change their garments after ministering before the Lord in the holy place. They were not allowed to reenter the outer court wearing the holy garments which they wore in the holy place. These garments could not come into direct contact with the people.

Measurements of the Entire Temple Area (42:15-20)

After completing the measurements of the interior of the Temple area, the man led Ezekiel out by way of the east gate. Then he measured the outer dimensions of the wall around the entire Temple complex. It was a perfect square, five hundred cubits on each side. The wall around the Temple served to preserve the separateness between the holiness of the Temple and the commonness of everything else. The Old Testament constantly maintains the distinction between the holy and the common as a reminder of the holiness of God.

The Return of the Glory of the Lord (43:1-5)

It had been almost nineteen years since Ezekiel had witnessed in a vision the departure of the glory of the Lord from Jerusalem (11:22-24). Now, with the measuring of the new Temple completed, God was ready to return to his people.

In an obvious parallel to the departure, Ezekiel witnessed in this vision the return of the Lord's glory from the same direction the Lord had gone when he abandoned Jerusalem (v. 2). The experience affected Ezekiel very much like his visions described in chapters

1—3 and 8—11 (v. 3). As he had done at the river Chebar, he was so overwhelmed that he fell on his face.

The Lord's glory entered the Temple by the east gate. Then the Spirit transported Ezekiel to the inner court where he saw the glory of the Lord fill the Temple, as it had done at the dedication of Solomon's Temple (1 Kings 8:10-11). Ezekiel understood that the years of the Lord's disfavor toward his people were coming to an end.

The Voice of God from the Temple (43:6-12)

Ezekiel heard the Lord's voice from within the Temple. God told the prophet that his presence was going to dwell in the midst of his people forever (v. 7). Never again would they defile the holy name of God by their idolatry. Nor would they make the Temple unclean by locating their royal tombs or the royal palace near the Temple.

The Lord instructed Ezekiel to describe the new Temple to the people exactly as he had seen it in the vision. When they knew that God was willing to make a fresh start with them and to dwell once again in their midst, surely they would be ashamed of all the sins they had committed (v. 10). Not only was Ezekiel instructed to describe the new Temple to them, but he was to make a written account of the vision (v. 11). In addition, the Lord told Ezekiel to inform the people that he had designated all the territory around the new Temple as holy.

The Altar of Burnt Offering (43:13-27)

A focal point of worship for the Israelites in the Temple was the altar of burnt offering (Ex. 20:24-26; 27:1-8). There they brought their animals to be sacrificed according to the regulations provided in the Mosaic law code. The importance of the altar in the new Temple is indicated by the special attention given to it in these verses.

Description of the altar (43:13-17).—The new altar will not be a reproduction of the altar described in Exodus 27:1-8. It will be in three square sections like terraces, or receding layers of a wedding cake, one above the other. Each section will be shorter than the section below it. The entire structure will be built on a foundation platform. The top section is the altar hearth, twelve cubits square. The total height, not including the foundation platform or the horns at each corner of the hearth, is ten cubits, the same height as Solomon's altar (2 Chron. 4:1). The altar hearth will be reached by steps on the east side, although steps were not allowed in the original altar (v. 17; see Ex. 20:26).

Consecration of the altar (43:18-27).—The Lord explained the procedure for cleansing the altar so it would be fit for offering burnt offerings on it. Only the Levitical priests of the family of Zadok will be allowed to minister at the altar (v. 19). To consecrate the altar, they will bring a bull for a sin offering and cleanse the altar by putting some of the bull's blood on the horns and other designated places. Then the bull will be burned outside the sacred Temple area (v. 21). The next day the same procedure will be repeated with a he-goat (v. 22). When the cleansing is completed, a bull and a ram, both without blemish, will be offered as burnt offerings after sprinkling salt on them. Salt was a symbol of fidelity in the ancient world (compare Num. 18:19).

For seven days a goat, a bull, and a ram will be offered in order to complete the consecration of the altar. Beginning on the eighth day, the priests can then accept the people's animals for burnt offerings and peace offerings on the altar (v. 27).

The Hebrew word for "consecrate" the altar (v. 26) literally means "to fill the hand." It originally referred to the offerings that they brought to the altar and placed in the hands of priests.

Earlier God had said that the people's sacrifices were an abomination to him and would not make him favorably disposed toward them (Isa. 1:12-15). Now he encouraged them that when the new altar is completed and properly consecrated, "I will accept you" (v. 27).

Regulations for Worship in the New Temple (44:1 to 46:24)

Even as instructions had been given in great detail for worshiping the Lord when the Tabernacle was built, regulations for worship in the new Temple are now given.

The Closed East Gate (44:1-3)

After the Lord returns to the new Temple through the outer gate on the east side (43:4), it will be too sacred for human feet to tread on the same ground. Therefore, the Lord told Ezekiel that the east gate will remain shut thereafter (44:2). No one can enter by that gate. The shut gate would also seem to suggest a promise from God that he will not leave the Temple again.

The only person allowed in the gate will be the prince. He may sit there to eat bread (v. 3). The prince has been identified variously as (1) King David; (2) a descendant of David, who is the reigning king; and (3) the Messiah. Although the identification of the prince as the Messiah is quite ancient, he seems to be a human being in 46:16; and in 45:22 he offers a sin offering for himself. Thus, there are some problems with equating the prince of these verses with the Messiah.

Regulations for Admission to the Temple (44:4-31)

One of God's accusations against his people before Jerusalem's destruction was their failure to preserve the sanctity of the Temple (see Ezek. 8). Such carelessness will not be tolerated in the new Temple.

The exclusion of foreigners (44:4-9).—The influence of foreign gods had been a stumbling block to the Hebrew people from their earliest history (see, for example, Num. 25:1-3; 33:50-56; Josh. 24:14; Hos. 7:14-16; Jer. 10:1-10; Ezek. 20:8). They had not only allowed foreign deities to be worshiped in the Temple (ch. 8), they had even put foreigners in charge of the sanctuary (v. 8). The Lord ordered them never again to admit uncircumcised foreigners into his sanctuary (v. 9).

It should be clearly understood that the condemnation of foreigners in the Old Testament is not based on racial prejudice but on the concern for purity of worship. Foreigners were accepted in Israel if they accepted the Lord as their God (as, for example, Ruth, a Moabitess). More often, however, they brought their gods into the land and enticed the Hebrews to worship their gods (Deut. 7:4). Israel's past tragedy had largely been the result of pagan influences on her people.

Temple duties assigned to the Levites (44:10-14).—With foreigners prohibited from entering the Temple to perform any services in it, those duties will be restored to the Levites (v. 11). However, the Levites will be punished for their past idolatry by not being allowed to perform priestly duties (v. 13). They will be limited to menial tasks that are required in the new Temple, such as guarding the gates and slaying the animals for sacrifice.

Priestly duties assigned to the Zadokites (44:15-31).—Only the Zadokites will be allowed to come near the Lord to perform priestly duties in the new Temple (vv. 15-16). Zadok was descended from Aaron (1 Chron. 6:50-53) and was a priest in David's time (2 Sam. 8:17; 15:24-29). Solomon appointed him to replace Abiathar as the chief priest (1 Kings 2:26-27,35). Descendants of Zadok continued to serve as high priests until 171 BC, when Menelaus, a Benjamite, was made high priest by offering a large sum of money for the position to the ruler, Antiochus IV (Epiphanes).

Historically, there was an ongoing struggle between the Zadokite and Levitical priests for control of the priesthood. The Levites seemed to have gained control in the post-Exilic period in spite of Ezekiel's elevation of the Zadokites. However, by New Testament times, the Zadokites had regained control. They were known then as the Sadducees.

The priests will be required to wear linen garments when they enter the inner court (v. 17). In order to avoid ritual uncleanness, no wool or anything that might cause them to sweat can be worn. When they return to the outer court after performing their priestly duties, they will be required to remove the sacred linen garments and put on other clothes. This will be done to prevent holiness from being transmitted to the people.

Other regulations governing the priests include the length of their hair to avoid the appearance of being in mourning (v. 20), abstinence from wine when going into the inner court to perform their priestly duties (v. 21; see Lev. 10:9), and whom they can marry (v. 22; Lev. 21:14). All these regulations are intended to instruct the people concerning the differences between the holy and the common. In all respects the priests are to be examples of separateness and are to teach the people the difference between the holy and the common by their lives.

Additional duties of the priests will include serving as judges in the disputes of the people and observing the feast days and the sabbath (v. 24). They cannot defile themselves by going near a corpse except in the case of the death of a member of their immediate family (v. 25). This regulation contrasts with the Nazirite vow, that prohibited the Nazirite from touching the corpse of anyone, including family members (Num. 6:6-7). If a priest does defile himself by contact with a corpse, he cannot minister in the

Temple for seven days after he is cleansed (vv. 26-27).

Priests will not be given an inheritance in the land, as the Lord is their only possession (v. 28; compare Num. 18:20; 35:2). In other words, they will own no land upon which they can grow grain and fruit or graze animals to supply their food. Their food will be provided through the offerings brought by the people (v. 30). They will not be allowed to eat the meat of any bird or animal that died of itself or has been mangled by another animal (v. 31). This last prohibition will apply to all Israelites (Lev. 7:24).

Allotment of the Land (45:1-8)

Even as the land had been divided by allotment when the Israelites entered Canaan under Joshua's leadership (Josh. 13—22), there will be another allotment in the restored nation. A holy district will be set apart that measures twenty-five thousand cubits long and twenty thousand cubits wide. Within that district, a square area of five hundred cubits will be set aside as the sanctuary with an open space of fifty cubits around it (v. 2; see 42:20). The sanctuary will be located in a section of the holy district twenty-five thousand cubits long and ten thousand cubits wide. That part of the holy district will be allotted to the priests for their homes and for the sanctuary (v. 4). Another section of equal size will be set apart for the Levites to live in (v. 5).

The remaining portion of the holy district will belong to the entire house of Israel for them to live in. Jerusalem will be located in this area (v. 6).

On the east and west sides of the land that is set apart as the holy district (described above in vv. 1-6), land will be designated for the prince. North to south, it will correspond in width to the combined widths of the land set apart for the priests, Levites, and the city (that is, twenty-five thousand cubits). On the west it will extend from the holy district to the Mediterranean Sea. On the east it will extend from the holy district to the Jordan River. The purpose of such a generous portion of the land for the prince is to prevent any further desire by the princes to take the people's land from them (v. 8).

Responsibilities of the Princes (45:9-17)

A warning to be honest (45:9-12).—The leaders of Judah had largely been responsible for the downfall of their nation. They had been greedy, immoral, dishonest, and oppressors of their people. Most of them were not examples of righteousness before their people. The Lord insisted that the future leaders must change their ways.

The Lord had had enough of the violence and oppression of the princes. In the future they must practice justice and righteousness and never evict the people from the land. God ordered them to use honest scales in the marketplace (compare Amos 8:5).

Offerings of the prince (45:13-17).—Verses 13-15 enumerate the offerings that the people are to bring to the prince to be used for grain offerings, burnt offerings, drink, and peace offerings. From these offerings it will be the prince's duty to furnish the offerings and sacrifices for all the appointed feasts.

The Festival Calendar (45:18-25)

The remainder of chapter 45 records the dates on which certain religious ceremonies and festivals are to be observed. On the first day of the first month a young bull will be sacrificed for purification of the Temple. Some of its blood from the sin offering is to be put on the doorposts of the Temple, on the altar of burnt offering, and on the posts of the gate of the inner court. The same ritual is to be repeated on the seventh day of the month for anyone who has sinned through error or ignorance. (Most commentators believe that the first day of the seventh month is intended rather than the seventh day of the first month.)

On the fourteenth day of the first month the Passover will be observed (see Ex. 12:6), followed by the Feast of Unleavened Bread for seven days (v. 21; see Ex. 12:15). The prince will be required to provide sacrificial offerings for the sin and burnt offerings and for the grain offering during the Feasts of Passover and Unleavened Bread. He will also provide the offerings for the Feast of Tabernacles on the fifteenth day of the seventh month.

Other Regulations for the Prince and the Temple (46:1-24)

Chapter 46 contains a collection of miscellaneous regulations that involve both the prince and the Temple. There is no single, unifying emphasis in the chapter.

Regulations for worship on holy days (46:1-7).—The east gate to the inner court will be kept closed every day except on the day of the sabbath and the new moon. On those days it will be opened, and the prince will come and stand at the entrance to the gateway. There he will have the privilege of watching the priests perform their duties at the altar, although he cannot enter the inner court himself. The people can also worship at the entrance of that gate on the days of the sabbath and the new moon festival. The offerings are prescribed that the prince will bring on both those holy days for burnt offerings and grain offerings (vv. 4-7).

The offerings on both occasions will be the same, except that on the day of the new moon a young bull and an ephah of flour will be added (vv. 6-7). The amounts are different from those prescribed in the Mosaic law (see Num. 28:9-15).

The festival of the new moon fell on the first day of the month. Many Hebrew religious festivals were calculated on a lunar basis. The Feasts of Passover (including Pentecost fifty days later) and Tabernacles were calculated on the basis of the appearance of the new moon of the month in which they occurred. Easter and the Christian Pentecost are still determined by a lunar calculation, which causes the dates on which they fall to vary each year.

Regulations for entering and leaving the Temple (46:8-10).—The prince will enter and leave the Temple by the same gate. However, when the people come to worship at the time of the appointed feasts, they will not go out by the gate they entered. If they enter by the north gate, they will exit through the south gate. If they enter by the south gate, they will exit through the north gate. This regulation will prevent confusion and preserve an orderly movement of the worshipers through the Temple on the days when great numbers of them will be there.

Verse 10 has been understood to mean that on the nonfestival days the prince will be treated like one of the people and enter and leave in the same way they do. It has also been interpreted to mean that the prince and the people are united in their worship of the Lord; that is, both will participate in the ceremonies at the same time.

Regulations for various offerings (46:11-15).—At the major festivals and on fixed occasions (such as the sabbath and the new moon), the amount of the grain offering is prescribed. It is an ephah of flour with a young bull or ram and as many lambs as a person is able to give, together with a hin of oil for each ephah of flour.

When the prince wishes to make a freewill offering, one that is not required by the law, the east gate will be opened for him; and he will bring his freewill offering through the east gate, just as he does on the sabbath. When he leaves, the east gate will be shut again.

The prince will also provide a daily offering each morning. It will consist of a year-old lamb for a burnt offering and one-sixth of an ephah of flour and one-third of a hin of oil mixed in the flour for a grain offering.

There is no mention of evening offerings, as found elsewhere in the Old Testament (see Ex. 29:38-41; Num. 28:3-8; 2 Kings 16:15).

Regulations for the prince's gifts of land (46:16-18).—The prince will be allowed to make gifts to his sons from his land inheritance. The land will be their property by right of inheritance. However, if he makes a gift of land to any of his servants, it will not be in perpetuity. It can be held only until the "year of liberty," that is, the year when bondservants are to be released according to the law (v. 17; see Ex. 21:2-11; 23:10-11; Lev. 25:44-46; Deut. 15:1,12-18; Jer. 34:14). When the servant is freed, the gift will be returned to the prince. We would call such a practice "Indian giving," but the purpose of the regulation is to safeguard the prince's inheritance and keep it within the family.

The prince will not be permitted to take away forcibly the property of any of his subjects (as Ahab did, 1 Kings 21:1-16; see also Amos 2:6-7; Isa. 5:8). Whatever property he gives to his sons as their inheritance must come from his own property. By this regulation, the property rights of the common people will be protected.

Regulations for cooking in the Temple (46:19-24).—In these verses we return to the conducted tour of the new Temple that began in chapter 40. Ezekiel was taken to the north row of priests' chambers in the inner court. At the western extremity of those chambers he was shown the place where the priests will boil the guilt and sin offerings and bake the grain offerings. The priests will not be allowed to take any of these offerings into the outer court, lest they communicate holiness to the people.

Though not specifically stated, there must have been a similar place for cooking on the south side of the inner court.

Then Ezekiel was escorted to the outer court where he was shown cooking areas in each of the four corners of the outer court. Each one was the same size. In those areas the Levites will boil the sacrifices that the people bring to them. Thus worship, sacrifice, cooking, and eating will merge in one place—the Temple!

Description of the Transformed Land (47:1 to 48:35)

The man who escorted Ezekiel through the Temple then brought him back to the entrance of the Temple on its east side. The rest of the vision focuses on the land and on the city, including a river that will flow from the Temple.

Life-Giving Waters from the Temple (47:1-12)

Ezekiel saw water flowing from below the threshold of the Temple at its south end. It flowed eastward by way of the south side of the altar. The man escorted Ezekiel out the north gate around to the outer gate on the east side. There he could see the water coming out on the south side of the gate. Continuing eastward, the man led Ezekiel a thousand cubits to where the water was ankle deep. They continued another thousand cubits and found that the water came to their knees. They walked another thousand cubits, and the water was up to their loins. They walked another thousand cubits, and Ezekiel found the water had become a river too deep to pass through. The man pointedly asked Ezekiel if he were carefully observing all that was being shown to him (v. 6).

As they walked back along the bank of the river, Ezekiel saw great numbers of trees growing on either side. The man informed Ezekiel that the river flowed eastward to the depression of the Jordan Valley called the Arabah. From there it flowed down to the Dead Sea, an unusual body of water so filled with salt and other minerals that neither plant nor animal life can live in it. However, when the waters of the river mingle with the waters of the Dead Sea, the sea will become fresh water and teem with fish. The Dead Sea will become a fisherman's paradise. Villages around the sea will be populated with people who make their living fishing.

The waters of the swamps and marshes around the sea will not become fresh (v. 11). They will continue to provide salt and other valuable minerals. Growing on either side of the river will be all kinds of fruit trees. Their leaves will never wither, and they will bear fresh fruit every month. Their fruit will provide an abundant source of food for the people, and their leaves will be used for medicinal purposes.

Many lessons can be derived from this beautiful picture of the life-giving waters that will flow from the Temple: (1) It reminds us that God is the one who can turn death into life. (2) Sometimes God begins his work in small and ordinary ways. (3) God is the source of all blessings. (4) God's blessings flow from him to all parts of the world and are abundant and unending. (5) The power of God can transform everything it touches. Revelation 22:1-2 evidently builds on the description of the river that Ezekiel saw and calls it "the river of the water of life."

Boundaries of the Land (47:13-21)

The division of the transformed land among the twelve tribes will not be on the same basis as it was in Joshua's time. The land is to be divided equally among the twelve tribes with Joseph's tribe receiving two portions. As previously indicated, the tribe of Levi will not share in the land (44:28); so in order to maintain the number twelve, the tribes of Joseph's sons, Manasseh and Ephraim, will each receive a portion.

The geographical boundaries will begin somewhere near the seaport of Tyre in the north and extend eastward to the headwaters of the Jordan River southwest of Damascus (vv. 15-17; compare the boundary description given in Num. 34:1-12). Most of the places named cannot be identified with certainty. A Bible encyclopedia should be consulted for the possible location of each of the places named in these verses.

The eastern boundary is easier to identify. It will follow the Jordan river south to the Dead Sea (called in v. 18 the "eastern sea").

The southern boundary will extend from the Dead Sea southwestward to Meribath-kadesh (better known as Kadesh-barnea). Then it will go to the Brook of Egypt, known today as Wadi el-Arish. This river is not to be confused with the Nile River. The southern boundary will then follow the Brook of Egypt to the Mediterranean Sea.

The western boundary will follow the coastline of the Mediterranean back to the starting point in the north.

Division of the Land (47:22 to 48:35)

With the general boundaries of the land established, now the areas within the land are assigned to each tribe. The land given to seven of the tribes will lie to the north of the holy district, and the land for the remaining five tribes will be south of the holy district. The allotments are arbitrary and have no relationship to historico-geographical realities or to the size of the tribes.

Provision for the aliens (47:22-23).—A remarkable feature in the division of the land is the provision for the resident aliens who live there. They will receive their portion of land with the members of the tribes among whom they live (compare the regulations of Lev. 24:22; Num. 15:29; Isa. 56:3-8). Their right to hold land is not mentioned elsewhere in the Old Testament. Some commentators believe that these aliens are those who become proselytes to the Hebrew faith, but the passage does not say so. To allow them land is a bold and daring step forward in human relationships unknown in the ancient world.

Allotment for the seven northern tribes (48:1-7).—Seven of the tribes will be located north of the sacred district that is reserved for the Temple, the city, the priests, and the Levites. The seven are named in order according to their location north to south: Dan, Asher, Naphtali, Manasseh, Ephraim, Reuben, and Judah.

It is interesting to observe that the tribes descended from Jacob's concubines are located farthest away from the sacred sanctuary both on the north and south sides. On the north side from north to south Dan, Asher, and Naphtali will be located—all sons of concubines (Gen. 30:6,8,13). Next to them will be the tribes of Manasseh and Ephraim, the sons of Joseph. Reuben, Jacob's eldest son, is located next to Ephraim, and next to him is Judah.

Among the northern tribes Judah is given the place of honor immediately adjacent to the holy portion. Judah, Jacob's fourth son, had taken the place of the firstborn, Reuben, as the inheritor of the blessing of Jacob (Gen. 49:8-12).

Allotment for the central sacred portion (48:8-22).—Much of what is contained in verses 8-22 is an expansion of what has already been encountered in 45:1-8. These verses describe the sacred portion set apart for the sanctuary, the city, the priests, and the Levites. Its overall dimensions are twenty-five thousand cubits in width and twenty-five thousand cubits in length. Within this area, the Zadokite priests are to receive an allotment twenty-five thousand cubits long and ten thousand cubits wide (vv. 9-12).

Adjoining the allotment of the Zadokite priests to the north is a portion of equal size for the Levites, twenty-five thousand cubits long and ten thousand cubits wide (v. 13). The Levites cannot sell or exchange any of this land, for it is holy to the Lord (v. 14). It is assumed, though not stated, that the same restriction will hold regarding sale or exchange of their land.

The remaining part of the sacred portion, twenty-five thousand cubits in length and five thousand cubits in width, will be reserved for the city of Jerusalem, for dwellings, and for open land around the city. Jerusalem will be located in the midst of this area, occupying a square area of forty-five hundred cubits on each side. There will be two-hundred fifty cubits of open land on each side of the city. The remainder of the land will be cultivated to provide food for the workers who live in the city. The workers themselves will be responsible for tilling the land.

The area that remains on the east and west sides of the holy portion will belong to the prince (v. 21). It will reach to the Mediterranean Sea on the west and to the Jordan River on the east. This land area will be bordered by Judah on the north and by Benjamin on the south.

Allotment for the five southern tribes (48:23-29).—The five remaining tribes will be located south of the sacred portion that is reserved for the Temple, the city, the priests, and the Levites. These tribes are named in the order of their location from north to south: Benjamin, Simeon, Issachar, Zebulun, and Gad. Among the southern tribes, Benjamin, Rachel's son, is given the place of honor immediately adjacent to the holy portion. Simeon, Issachar, and Zebulun were sons of Leah and are listed next. Farthest away on the south side is Gad, the child of Jacob's concubine, Zilpah (Gen. 30:11).

The city of Jerusalem (48:30-35).—There will be twelve gates for the city of Jerusalem, three on each side. They are named after the twelve tribes. Since Levi has a gate named for him, Joseph replaces Ephraim and Manasseh in order to preserve the number twelve (vv. 31-32).

On the north are the gates named for Reuben, the firstborn son; Judah, who received Jacob's chief blessing and was the ancestor of David; and Levi, who became the priestly tribe.

On the east side are the gates named for Joseph, the father of Manasseh and Ephraim; Benjamin, Joseph's younger brother; and Dan, son of Rachel's maid named Bilhah. There is no apparent explanation for the grouping of the tribes on the east side, unless it is their relationship to Rachel.

On the south side are the gates named for Simeon, Issachar, and Zebulun, all of whom were sons of Leah (Gen. 29:33; 30:18-20).

On the west side are the gates named for Gad, Asher, and

Naphtali, all of whom were sons of concubines of Jacob (Gen. 30:8-13).

The description of the gates reminds us of the description of the gates of the new Jerusalem in Revelation 21:12-13. This passage also says that the twelve gates are named after the twelve tribes of Israel. In addition, it says new Jerusalem will have twelve foundation stones inscribed with the twelve names of the twelve apostles (Rev. 21:14).

In the closing and climactic verse of Ezekiel's Temple vision, Jerusalem is given a new name, "The Lord is there" (v. 35). The new name serves as a fitting grand finale for the Book of Ezekiel. Ezekiel had witnessed many things in the twenty-five years since his exile began. He had witnessed the departure of the glory of the Lord from the Temple. With God's protecting presence gone, the city was open for destruction in 587 BC by the Babylonians. Ezekiel was also aware of the hopelessness and despair that had gripped the survivors, both in Judah and those in exile.

There undoubtedly had been times during the years of exile when Ezekiel wondered if God's blessed presence would ever be restored to his people. Now that assurance has been given him through the vision of the new Temple. The covenant still stands. The Lord is their God, and they are still his people. He will dwell in the midst of his people forever, a people cleansed of their sins and their faithlessness.

Names of people were changed in ancient times to indicate a new relationship or to commemorate an important event. For example, Jacob's name was changed to Israel (Gen. 32:28). Ezekiel understood that because Jerusalem will be given a new name, a new relationship will be established someday between the Lord and his people. However, the new relationship remained only a vision for Ezekiel.

Ezekiel is not the only prophet who anticipated a new name for Jerusalem. Jeremiah said it will be called "The throne of the Lord" (Jer. 3:17). He said that it will also be called "The Lord is our righteousness" (Jer. 33:16). Zechariah said it will be called "The faithful city" (Zech. 8:3; "the City of Truth," NASB).

Although Ezekiel did not live to see the fulfillment of his vision, the apostle John, while in exile on the island of Patmos, did see it. He saw its fulfillment in the coming of Christ as the "Immanuel" of Isaiah 7:14 (the name means "God is with us"). There are some differences in the description of John's new Jerusalem and Ezekiel's, particularly the absence of a Temple in Revelation 21:22. However, in both visions, there is the assurance of God's presence with his people. "The throne of God and of the Lamb shall be in it, and his servants shall worship him; they shall see his face" (Rev. 22:3-4).

There are a number of verses in the visions of chapters 38—48 that are difficult to understand, but one message emerges in sharp focus through all these chapters. It is that the present evil world order is going to be brought to an end by God's direct intervention. He will establish a new order characterized by a holy, obedient people who worship him and enjoy fellowship with him. He will live in the midst of his people forever.

DANIEL

Introduction

The Book of Daniel is a paradox among the Scriptures. It is at the same time one of the best known and yet least understood of all the books of the Bible. Some of its stories, such as Daniel in the lions' den, are among the first Bible stories learned by children because they are so easy to understand. Other parts of the book, however, make use of a great deal of symbolic language, dreams, and visions; and scholars are still struggling to understand them.

There are two completely different ways of interpreting the Book of Daniel. At one extreme are those who see the book as a "map of the ages" or as a kind of crystal ball that reveals the events of world history to the end of time. At the other extreme are those who insist there is nothing predictive in the book. They say that the book describes events that took place during the time of successive Babylonian, Persian, and Greek rule over Judah until the re-establishment of Jewish independence around 165 BC.

Somewhere between these two attitudes toward the Book of Daniel are those who interpret parts of the book as historically fulfilled and other parts as yet unfulfilled.

A word of caution is in order for anyone who insists that his is the only correct interpretation of Daniel. Daniel himself was not as certain of the meaning of some of his visions as are some present-day Bible students. On one occasion he said, "I was appalled by the vision and did not understand it" (8:27). Therefore, we should not be reluctant to admit there are parts of the book we cannot understand.

A second word of caution needs to be stated before we embark on a study of Daniel. If someone does not agree with your interpretation of the book, do not conclude that he does not believe the Bible. It may only mean that he does not agree with your interpretation of Daniel.

Daniel the Man

During the third year of King Jehoiakim's reign, Nebuchadnezzar brought an army against Jerusalem to subdue a rebellion among the people (1:1). He took some plunder and some hostages to serve as warning to the people of Judah not to rebel again. The people taken by Nebuchadnezzar were not enslaved or imprisoned but were chosen rather for their ability and appearance for the purpose of being educated in Babylonian culture and wisdom. Daniel was among those chosen.

Nothing is known about Daniel except what is found in the book that bears his name which means "God is my judge." He was a young man of unusual intelligence, handsome in appearance, and a member of a noble family in Judah. We know this much about him because these were the qualities Nebuchadnezzar required of those who were chosen for his royal indoctrination (1:3-4).

Daniel's exile began in the third year of Jehoiakim's reign, which would be about 606 BC (see 1:1). He continued in royal service until at least 537 BC, the third year after the conquest of Babylon by Cyrus, king of Persia (10:1). He rose to great heights of power and influence during the reign of Nebuchadnezzar but seems to have lost royal favor by the time of Belshazzar's rule. He did not marry.

Daniel was a man of unusual courage and faith. He would not compromise his convictions for personal advancement or even at the risk of death. He had administrative ability that enabled him to become a high government official and royal adviser. He also had a remarkable ability to interpret dreams.

The Times in Which Daniel Lived

A large part of Daniel's life was lived during a period of crisis and discouragement for the people of Judah. The mighty Assyrian empire that had ruled the Near East for more than 135 years was overthrown in 612 BC by the Babylonians, who dominated the ancient Near East until they, in turn, were defeated by the Persians in 539 BC. Daniel was only a child when Assyria was overthrown, but he may have been aware of the foreboding and uncertainty in Judah caused by the power struggles that were taking place around his tiny homeland.

Early in his reign King Jehoiakim of Judah evidently gave some indication of rebellion against Babylon. As a result the Babylonians sent an army to Jerusalem to quell the revolt (see 2 Kings 24:1;

2 Chron. 36:5-8). It was at that time that Daniel was taken to Babylon to be educated in the wisdom of Babylon at Nebuchadnezzar's court. He was in Babylon when Jerusalem was destroyed by the Babylonians in 587 BC.

Daniel lived to see the fall of the Babylonian empire to the Persians in 539 BC. It is not impossible that he was a witness to the ceremony in which King Cyrus signed a decree that allowed the Jewish exiles to return to their own land (2 Chron. 36:22-23). Thus his life spanned an era of about eighty years that were among the most turbulent and significant in Jewish history.

Those who date Daniel or parts of it around 165 BC find a different setting for the book from the one just described. They believe the book was written when Antiochus IV (Epiphanes) ruled Syria, including Judah, from 175 to 164 BC. He was a cruel tyrant, almost to the degree of madness. He was determined to spread Greek culture throughout his domain, but the Jews stubbornly held to their Jewish traditions.

After a humiliating defeat at the hand of the Romans in Egypt in 168 BC, Antiochus took out his anger and frustration on the Jews. He ordered the destruction of Jerusalem and the death of any of its people who resisted. He abolished the Jewish laws and religious practices and compelled the Jews to take part in heathen festivals or be put to death. Open rebellion broke out in 167 BC led by the Maccabee family. The revolt was successful, and the Temple sacrifices were restored in 165 BC. Antiochus withdrew and died insane in Persia in 164 BC. He is the "king of bold countenance" and the "little horn" described in Daniel 8, in this interpretation.

The Book of Daniel

Although Daniel is considered to be a prophet, his book is not included with the books of the Prophets which form the second division of the Hebrew Bible. Instead, it is included in the third division, called the Writings, which includes such books as Psalms, 1 and 2 Chronicles, and Esther. The Septuagint translators (who made the first translation of the Old Testament into Greek) placed Daniel after the Book of Ezekiel, where it remains in our English language Bibles. Daniel is composed of two almost equal parts, chapters 1—6, which are largely biographical, and chapters 7—12, which contain Daniel's visions.

Although most of the Old Testament was originally written in the

Hebrew language, certain parts in the Hebrew Bible have been preserved in the Aramaic language, which is very much like Hebrew. These Aramaic portions are Ezra 4:8 to 6:18; 7:12-26; Jeremiah 10:11; and Daniel 2:4b to 7:28. Many explanations have been proposed by scholars for the use of Aramaic in Daniel, but none of them has found general acceptance.

Many Old Testament scholars believe that the Book of Daniel, or parts of it, was composed long after Daniel lived, probably around 165 BC. Conservative scholars continue to insist that the sixth-century BC date for Daniel is correct and that the book is a unity. The fact that the Book of Daniel was studied by the Qumran community in the first century BC needs to be given more consideration by scholars who insist that the book was written around 165 BC. If written that late, it is difficult to understand why it was so well known and apparently considered canonical so soon after it was written, as evidenced by the number of fragments and copies of the book found at Qumran.

More than any other book of the Old Testament, Daniel makes use of the apocalyptic style of writing (see the remarks on Ezekiel 38 for an explanation of apocalyptic).

Whether or not scholars will ever agree as to the meaning of certain details of the Book of Daniel, there is unanimous agreement that the purpose of the book is to give assurance of the triumph of God over all evil. This is a message that was surely needed by the defeated and scattered Jewish people in Daniel's time. It is a message that still needs to be heard and believed today.

Daniel and His Friends in Babylon
1:1 to 6:28

Four Young Men in a Foreign Royal Court (1:1-21)

Jehoiakim's short-lived revolt against Nebuchadnezzar in the third year of his reign resulted in a humiliating defeat for Jehoiakim and his people. The Babylonians sent an army that surrounded Jerusalem, and so the king apparently surrendered with little resistance. Nebuchadnezzar plundered the Temple of some of its vessels and removed them to the house of his god in Shinar (an ancient name for Babylon, also found in Gen. 10:10; 11:2).

Jehoiakim may have been taken to Babylon for a short time, then released and allowed to return to Jerusalem after giving ample assurance of his loyalty to Nebuchadnezzar (see 2 Chron. 36:5-8).

The King's Plan for Educating Jewish Exiles (1:1-7)

Along with the Temple vessels, the Babylonians took a number of choice young men to Babylon for the purpose of training them in the Babylonian language and culture for three years. They were chosen for their unexcelled physical appearance and superior intelligence. At the end of their training the king planned to place them in his service. As a part of their total immersion in Babylonian life, the king gave them the same rich food he ate and the wine he drank.

Among the young men were four from the tribe of Judah named Daniel ("God is my Judge"), Hananiah ("The Lord has been gracious"), Mishael ("Who is what God is"), and Azariah ("The Lord has helped"). As part of their total "Babylonization," they were given Babylonian names: Belteshazzar, Shadrach, Meshach, and Abed-nego. This was done not by their choice but for the convenience of the Babylonians and also as a reminder that they were under Babylonian authority. There is some uncertainty about the exact meaning of their Babylonian names, but several of the new names contain references to Babylonian deities.

Daniel's Refusal of the King's Food (1:8-16)

Kings were responsible for providing the meals served in their households, and it was a special honor to be served the same food that the king ate. However, Daniel determined that he would not eat the king's food or drink his wine, although he accepted a new name and a Babylonian education without complaint. Daniel's objections were religious, not health-related. He knew that to eat food that was unclean or was prepared in violation of the Mosaic dietary laws resulted in ceremonial defilement. Also, in pagan countries food was often offered to the gods before being served at a meal.

Daniel asked the chief of the eunuchs, named Ashpenaz, who was in charge of the young men, for permission not to defile himself with the king's food. The eunuch personally had no objections, but he was afraid that another diet would result in a poorer physical condition than that of those who ate the king's food. If this happened, the eunuch feared the king would hold him responsible and order his execution.

Daniel proposed a test for ten days, during which time he and his three friends would be given a diet of water and "vegetables" (from a word that means *seeds*). Then the steward appointed by the chief eunuch could compare their appearance with the appearance of those who ate the king's food and make his decision whether they could continue their diet. The steward consented to the test, and at the end of the ten days it was apparent that Daniel and his friends were healthier than the others. The steward then allowed the four friends to continue eating the food they preferred.

God was with the four young men because of their faithfulness to him. He gave them unusual learning and wisdom. In addition, Daniel was given understanding in visions and dreams which would serve him well later. It took a great deal of courage to refuse the king's food and wine. The king could have taken offense at their refusal and ordered their execution.

Their dedication was even more remarkable when it is remembered that they were far away from home, free from parental and family authority, and free to do as they pleased. They could have argued that since God had not prevented their deportation to Babylon, they were not obligated to obey his wishes. But they chose not to depart from the faith they had practiced from childhood or to compromise their convictions. How many young people today maintain the same faithfulness when they leave home for the first time?

Outcome of the Test (1:17-21)

At the end of the three years all the young men of Judah who had been subjected to the king's training were brought before him. It was obvious that Daniel and his three friends were superior in every way, so Nebuchadnezzar gave them responsible positions in his court (this is the meaning of "they stood before the king," v. 19). The king even discovered to his surprise that the four friends were infinitely superior to his own magicians and enchanters.

The chapter closes with a statement that Daniel remained in Babylon until the first year of the reign of Cyrus, the Persian ruler who successfully overthrew the Babylonian empire in 539 BC (v. 21).

Nebuchadnezzar's Dream About a Statue (2:1-49)

In the ancient world dreams were considered to be supernatural in origin; therefore, they were accorded a great deal of importance. Kings based major decisions on dreams, for they believed the dreams came from the gods. There were many professional interpreters of dreams both in the royal courts and among the common people. The meanings of dreams were systematized and compiled into books that could be consulted by soothsayers.

In the Bible dreams are frequently employed as a means of God's revelation (for example, Gen. 40:9-19; 41:1-24; Num. 12:6; 1 Sam. 28:6; 1 Kings 3:5-15; Matt. 1:20-21). But, at the same time, warnings are given that dreams may not be from God (for example, Deut. 13:1-5; Jer. 23:32; 27:9; Zech. 10:2).

An Impossible Demand (2:1-11)

In the second year of Nebuchadnezzar's reign (that is, 603 BC), he had dreams that troubled him so much that he could not sleep. The Hebrew of verse 1 says he could not sleep because "his spirit pushed itself." Therefore, he summoned all the magicians, enchanters, sorcerers, and Chaldeans and demanded that they tell him his dream. The king had never made such a difficult demand, and they were obviously frightened.

The Chaldeans, famous for their expertise in magical lore, served as spokesmen for the group. They assured him that if he would tell them the dream, they could interpret it. The king angrily responded that he would have them torn limb from limb and their houses destroyed if they did not tell him both the dream and its interpretation. At the same time he promised to reward them handsomely if they could tell him the dream and then interpret it!

It is not certain whether Nebuchadnezzar had really forgotten the dream or whether he was testing the soothsayers' ability as dream interpreters by not telling them the dream. It seems that he would not have known whether their account of the dream was correct unless he remembered it. If they could tell him the dream, he would be assured that their interpretation was correct! Whether he knew the dream or not did not lessen the dilemma of the soothsayers.

Their continued pleas for him to reveal the dream only convinced the king that they were frauds. Their insistence that only the gods could do what he asked increased his rage. He issued a decree that all the wise men in the land were to be slain. Unfortunately for Daniel and his friends, the decree included them also.

Daniel's Offer to Interpret the Dream (2:12-30)

Upon learning of the decree, Daniel approached Arioch, the "captain of the king's guard" (literally, "chief of the slaughterers"), who had been placed in charge of the executions. He asked for an explanation of the severity of the king's decree. After Arioch told him what had happened, Daniel petitioned the king to set a time for Daniel to interpret his dream.

Daniel told his three friends what had happened and asked them to join him in prayer that God would reveal the dream to him so that they would not perish (v. 18).

God came to Daniel in a vision at night and revealed the mysterious dream to him, whereupon Daniel expressed his gratitude in an eloquent prayer of praise and thanksgiving (vv. 20-23).

Daniel went again to Arioch and asked him to take him to the king so that he could interpret the king's dream. Arioch escorted Daniel with haste to the king, for it is certain that everyone in the court was feeling the king's ill humor and wished to see the matter ended.

The Interpretation of the Dream (2:31-45)

Daniel boldly acknowledged to Nebuchadnezzar that it was his God who reveals mysteries (v. 28). He was careful to disclaim any ability of his own to interpret the king's dreams (v. 30).

He told the king that he had dreamed about a colossal statue in human form that was made of various metals and clay (vv. 32-33). A stone not cut by human hands smashed the statue into small pieces that were then carried away by the wind. The stone then grew until it became a mountain that filled the whole earth.

Daniel explained that the parts of the statue made of different metals represented a succession of four kingdoms. The stone represented the kingdom of God that would eventually replace all the earthly kingdoms and endure forever.

Daniel's Reward (2:46-49)

The king was overwhelmed by Daniel's ability to interpret his dream and fell before him. He was prepared to worship Daniel with an offering and incense. He acknowledged that Daniel's God was "God of gods and Lord of kings" (v. 47). His praise of God does not mean that he became a convert to the Jewish faith, for in his polytheistic culture he was only adding another god to those he already believed in.

Nebuchadnezzar lavished honors and gifts on Daniel and made him ruler over the whole province of Babylon and chief over all the wise men. In his time of elevation Daniel did not forget his three friends. He asked the king to put them in charge of the affairs of the province of Babylon, and the request was granted. Daniel remained in the king's court (literally, "in the gate of the king," v. 49).

There is no disagreement among Bible students as to the general thrust of the dream and its interpretation. Its clear meaning is that all human kingdoms will pass away, but God's kingdom will remain forever. However, there is divided opinion concerning the identity of the kingdoms. One group says the successive kingdoms are Babylon, Medo-Persia, Greece, and Rome. The other says the kingdoms are Babylon, Media, Persia, and Greece. The essential point of contention between the two interpretations is that the first group believes the fourth kingdom includes a "revived" Roman empire and therefore anticipates the end of the present age. The second group believes that the four kingdoms have already been fulfilled historically.

There is a subtle irony in this chapter that is usually overlooked because of the focus on the identity of the kingdoms. Human wisdom is exposed as shallow and fraudulent in comparison to the wisdom given by God. The panic-stricken soothsayers, stripped of their pretense of wisdom, stand in sharp contrast to the poised, confident faith of Daniel.

Daniel's Friends in the Fiery Furnace (3:1-30)

The focus of the Book of Daniel is upon Daniel himself, but in chapter 3 he is not mentioned at all. The chapter records a single experience of his three friends that merits their inclusion among the "heroes of faith" of the Bible. The writer of Hebrews 11 may have had them in mind when he referred to those who "quenched raging fire" (Heb. 11:34). The story ranks among the most familiar narratives of the Old Testament.

The King's Edict (3:1-7)

Ancient rulers were frequently vain, cruel, and unreasonable. Nebuchadnezzar was no exception. He exercised the power of life and death over his subjects and expected instant compliance with his slightest whim.

For reasons not stated, he had a statue of gold made that was about ninety feet high and nine feet wide. It may have been an image of the king himself. The immense size probably means that the statue was overlaid with gold rather than made of solid gold. Nebuchadnezzar ordered it to be set up on the plain of Dura, a city whose exact location is unknown, but it was near the capital. It is possible there was some connection between this statue and the one in his dream (see ch. 2).

The king assembled all his officials for the dedication of the statue, including the satraps who ruled over the Babylonian provinces, down to the lowest officials in the land. A royal edict was read before the assembled dignitaries, ordering everyone in the kingdom to fall down and worship the golden statue at a given signal played on musical instruments. The list of musical instruments in verse 5 reminds us of the sophisticated cultural level attained by the ancient Babylonians. Some of the instruments have been identified, but some are still unknown today.

The edict further stated that anyone who refused to bow at the signal would be cast into a burning fiery furnace. The furnace was a type that was widely used in Babylon for making bricks.

Accusation Against the Friends (3:8-15)

The rapid rise of Daniel and his friends to power must have provoked intense jealousy and hatred in court circles. It is quite possible that the enemies of Daniel and his friends, knowing that the Jews would not comply, influenced the king to make the edict (as they did in 6:1-9). These enemies included Chaldeans who should have been grateful that Daniel's ability to interpret the king's dream had saved their lives.

Whether they were responsible for the edict concerning the statue or not, the enemies did not have to wait long for its violation by Shadrach, Meshach, and Abednego. Some of the Chaldeans immediately rushed to the king to inform him that the three Jewish friends had refused to bow before the golden statue. The Hebrew for "maliciously accused" (v. 8) is literally "ate the pieces."

Nebuchadnezzar was not accustomed to being defied and reacted with predictable rage. He ordered that the three Jews be brought before him so he could hear from their own lips whether they had refused to worship the statue. He reminded them of the penalty for violating his edict (v. 15).

The Friends' Defense (3:16-18)

The friends' reply is one of the most remarkable affirmations of faith to be found in the Scriptures. Their faith was comparable to that of Abraham, who was willing to sacrifice his own son if God required it (Gen. 22). With scorn for the consequences they informed the king that their God was able to deliver them from the king and from the fiery furnace itself. Such an answer in the presence of a monarch who had absolute authority over the lives of his subjects was extremely courageous and demonstrated their faith, but their next words were an even more profound expression of their faith. They added that even if God did not deliver them from the fire, they would not worship the golden statue (v. 18).

The faith of Shadrach, Meshach, and Abednego was not dependent on favorable circumstances like that of some people who are "fair-weather" believers. They affirm their love for God if things are going well, but if calamity or misfortune strikes them, they may turn and blame God for their distress. Genuine faith is the "in-spite-of-circumstances" kind expressed in Habakkuk 3:17-18. The three friends had the "in-spite-of" kind of faith that was not dependent on physical deliverance from the king's wrath.

A Harmless Fiery Furnace (3:19-30)

Their refusal to yield only angered the king more. He ordered the furnace to be heated seven times the usual temperature and to cast the men bound and clothed into the fire. The flames that leaped from the furnace consumed the soldiers who cast the three into the fire (v. 22).

Nebuchadnezzar was astonished to see a fourth person in the fire and that none of them was harmed by the flames. He said the appearance of the fourth person was like a "son of the gods," that is, some kind of supernatural being (v. 25; see also v. 28). He realized that the supernatural being was protecting the Jews from harm. The King James Version translates the expression as "the Son of God," which would suggest an appearance of Jesus in the furnace; this was an ancient interpretation of the church. How the pagan king could identify Jesus, who had not yet been incarnated, would be difficult to explain except as a unique revelation. Either translation can be justified because the word can properly be translated as a singular Hebrew word, *God,* or as a plural word, *gods.* However, the Aramaic equivalent is always plural, unless this is one exception.

The king ordered their immediate release. All those present saw that the flames did not harm their bodies or their clothing. The pagan king acknowledged that their God had delivered them and issued a decree, making the worship of their God lawful. He warned that anyone who even spoke a word against the Jews would be torn limb from limb and his house destroyed. As further evidence of his newfound respect for Shadrach, Meshach, and Abednego, he promoted them to higher positions in the province of Babylon. Their enemies' plot to see them destroyed had backfired, and now the Jews were in even higher favor with the king.

This story of courageous faith in the face of unjustified persecution has been a source of strength through the centuries for Jews and anyone else who has experienced persecution for his faith.

Nebuchadnezzar's Dream About a Tree (4:1-37)

Chapter 4 contains the account of Nebuchadnezzar's second dream. The time of the dream is not stated, but it may have been near the end of his reign, as his great building program seems to have been completed (v. 30). Again Daniel is the interpreter of the dream. The narrative is presented in the first person as a kind of public confession of how the king's pride was punished by God.

The King's Dream (4:1-18)

Couched in the form of a message to all his subjects, Nebuchadnezzar began by confessing the greatness and the kingship of the "Most High God" (v. 2). This name for God is found approximately forty-three times in the Old Testament and was often used by non-Jews (Gen. 14:18-20; Num. 24:16; Isa. 14:14). It stresses the omnipotence and exalted, transcendent majesty of God.

The king recalled a time when all was going well, and he was content and prosperous. His sense of well-being was interrupted by a dream that frightened him. He summoned all his wise men and told them the dream, but they could not interpret it. Daniel, whom the king called the "chief of the magicians" (v. 9), was then summoned, and the king told him his dream. The dream was about a great tree whose height reached from earth to heaven and could be seen everywhere. It had abundant fruit and provided nourishment and shade for everyone who was in its domain.

He then saw an angelic being, called a "watcher, a holy one" (v. 13), who gave orders to cut down the tree, leaving only the stump that was bound with a metal band. The dream seemed to shift from the symbolism of a tree to a person, as the angel then said, "Let a beast's mind be given to him; and let seven times pass over him" (v. 16).

Daniel's Interpretation of the Dream (4:19-27)

Daniel appeared to be upset by the dream and hesitated to tell the king its meaning. With the king's encouragement, Daniel explained that the tree represented the king, who had become great and powerful. The cutting down of the tree represented a decree from God to punish the king by forcing him to live like an animal for seven "times" (a word that probably means "years," but some think it means "seasons"). The stump served as a pledge that the kingdom was going to be restored to Nebuchadnezzar.

Daniel then appealed to the king to stop sinning and to show mercy to the oppressed in order to postpone or nullify the punishment.

Fulfillment of the Dream (4:28-37)

The king must have ignored Daniel's appeal to humble himself, for a year later, as he was walking on the palace roof, the king was stricken while boasting about the great empire he had built by his own efforts. Even as he was exulting in his greatness, a voice from heaven pronounced the beginning of his punishment. He developed a malady, the identity of which is uncertain. Because of superstitious fear, he was driven away from all human association and began to live and act like an animal. His malady has been identified as a form of insanity called lycanthropy, which causes a person to imagine himself to be an animal and to act like one. In support of the historicity of his illness, a Babylonian inscription has been found that says he was ill for four years. Ancient historians such as Berossus and Eusebius also mention his illness.

At the end of the period of punishment, Nebuchadnezzar acknowledged God ("lifted my eyes to heaven," v. 34), and the illness left him. He was restored to his throne and completed his reign that spanned forty-three years. He became even greater than before the illness, but he was careful to honor God and to remain humble before him.

Nebuchadnezzar's submission to God does not mean he abandoned his other gods; it only means he added another god to those in whom he already believed. The narrative teaches that pride will be punished and that the purpose of punishment is to lead to repentance.

There are some similarities between this story and an account of Nabonidus, the last king of Babylon and father of Belshazzar, who was serving as regent for his father in Babylon at the time of its fall. A "Prayer of Nabonidus," found in Cave 4 at Qumran, describes an inflammation that lasted for seven years. During that time Nabonidus was isolated from human society. He confessed his sins and was healed and then gave thanks to God. The similarities have caused some scholars to conclude that somehow the story of Nabonidus's illness was transferred to Nebuchadnezzar.

Belshazzar's Feast (5:1-31)

For years many critical scholars objected to the historicity of the reference to Belshazzar as the last king of Babylon (5:1) and as the son of Nebuchadnezzar (5:2,11). Actually, Nabonidus, Belshazzar's father, was Babylon's last king and a usurper who was not a descendant of Nebuchadnezzar. However, the first part of the problem has been solved by archaeological discoveries that show Belshazzar served as regent during the final years of Nabonidus's reign. It is not certain whether Nabonidus was indifferent to his kingly responsibilities or whether political enemies drove him into exile.

The identification of Nebuchadnezzar as Belshazzar's "father" offers no serious problem because in Hebrew and Aramaic "father" can mean "grandfather," "ancestor," or various kinds of relationships. For example, "sons of Belial" (1 Sam. 2:12, KJV and Hebrew) is used to describe any worthless person. King Joash called the prophet Elisha "My father" as a title of respect (2 Kings 13:14; compare 2 Kings 2:12).

Mysterious Handwriting on the Wall (5:1-12)

Belshazzar could not have been unaware that the Persian armies were outside the city when he held a feast for a thousand of his lords (v. 1). Verse 2 adds that the wives and concubines were also present. The fact that he feasted at such a critical time reveals the corruption which pervaded the royal court. The weakness of the political leaders made the empire ripe for plucking. As further evidence of his degenerate character, Belshazzar used the sacred Temple vessels that Nebuchadnezzar had brought from Jerusalem for serving wine to his drunken guests and for "toasting" the gods (v. 3).

While the guests were drinking wine from the Temple vessels, the fingers of a man's hand mysteriously appeared and wrote words on the wall that terrified the king. The words were Aramaic and readable to the king, but he did not understand their significance. He hastily summoned the wise men to interpret the words, but they could not, even though he promised them great rewards. "The queen" probably refers to the queen mother. Notice that the king's "wives" were present at the banquet (v. 2). The queen mother remembered Daniel, who by now was either in disfavor or retired from public life. She encouraged her son to call for Daniel to interpret the writing.

Daniel's Interpretation of the Handwriting (5:13-29)

The king summoned Daniel and offered to make him third ruler in the empire if he could interpret the words. Daniel refused the honors offered him and took the opportunity to remind Belshazzar how God had humbled Nebuchadnezzar because of his pride (vv. 20-21; compare 4:33). He warned Belshazzar that using the Temple vessels for his drunken orgy showed he had learned nothing from Nebuchadnezzar's humiliating experience.

Then Daniel proceeded to interpret the writing. He told the king that the first word, "MENE" (from a word that means "to count"), meant that God had numbered the days of the kingdom and had brought it to an end. The second word, "TEKEL" (from a word that means "to weigh"), meant that the king had been weighed on the scales of God's justice and did not measure up. The third word, "PERES" (the word means "to divide"; another form of the word, "PARSIN," is used in v. 25), meant that the kingdom had been divided between the Medes and Persians. The king's immediate response to a message that announced his doom was to reward

Daniel by making him third ruler in the nation! In light of the fact
that the enemy was at that moment entering the city the honor was a
mockery.

The Fall of Babylon (5:30-31)

The combined armies of the Medes and Persians and their allies
entered the city with little resistance. Apparently the Babylonian
people were ready for a change of leadership, even if it meant
submitting to foreign rule. Belshazzar was killed, and Darius the
Mede assumed control of the nation at the age of sixty-two (v. 31).

The mention of Darius the Mede remains one of the unsolved
historical problems of the book, for Cyrus the Great ruled Persia
from 550 to 530; Babylon was taken during his reign in 539. Darius
did not become ruler until 522. The solutions for the problem have
been numerous. Some scholars insist that the mention of Darius
means the writer was confused about the reigns of the Persian kings.

Other solutions assume the historical integrity of the text. One of
them equates Darius with Cyrus. As justification, it is noted that
since Cyrus gained control of the Median empire in 550, one of his
titles was "king of the Medes." Still another solution argues that a
general called Ugbaru (also called Gobryes) led the Persian troops to
victory over Babylon in 539 but died three weeks later. Then
according to cuneiform texts a man named Gubaru (called Darius in
Daniel, according to this explanation) was appointed by Cyrus as
"governor of Babylon and the region beyond the river."

Another solution is that Darius is an otherwise unknown vassal
king who served Cyrus in the early part of his reign and led the
armies that took Babylon.

Perhaps the recovery of additional documents by archaeologists at
some future time will clarify the identity of the Darius who was
responsible for taking Babylon. Whoever he was, he was responsible
for toppling a great empire that had ruled the ancient Near East for
only about sixty-five years.

Daniel in the Lions' Den (6:1-28)

The story of Daniel in the lions' den is one of the best known
stories in the Bible. Children listen wide-eyed as their parents or
Sunday School teachers read it to them. The story is deceptively

simple and uncomplicated, yet it contains some profound theological insights. It teaches that God will honor and protect those who trust him. It also suggests that private devotional time spent with God is just as important as public worship. Finally, it demonstrates that a crisis reveals what kind of faith we really have (compare Abraham, Gen. 22).

The story shows some similarities with the deliverance of Daniel's friends in chapter 3 and with the deliverance of the Jewish people in the Book of Esther.

A Plot by Daniel's Enemies (6:1-9)

After the Persian conquest of Babylon, Darius reorganized the political structure of his kingdom. He appointed 120 satraps to rule in the various provinces throughout the empire. They in turn were answerable to three "presidents" (v. 2; "commissioners," NASB; "administrators," NIV; the word is a Persian word that means "chief"). One of the three was Daniel, now about eighty years of age. The fact that he was given such a responsible position in the new government indicates that his reputation for integrity and dependability was well known, even to the Persians.

Daniel quickly proved his ability to the satisfaction of the king, who decided to appoint him to a governing position above all others except himself. This decision provoked the jealousy of the other presidents and the satraps so they sought to find some grounds for destroying his influence with the king. They were unable to uncover any wrongdoing in Daniel and realized that their only hope for alienating him from the king must be sought in connection with his religion.

They devised a plan that would flatter the king without calling attention to their plot to discredit Daniel. They approached the king with a suggestion that he proclaim a law that anyone who petitioned any god or man for thirty days, except the king, would be cast into the lions' den (v. 7). They urged him to sign the decree which they had already prepared. Unaware of the real intent of the decree, the king signed the document, with the knowledge that according to Persian and Median law not even the king could revoke it.

Daniel's Response to the Plot (6:10-13)

When Daniel learned about the new law, he went to his house and prayed on his knees before an open window three times a day as he had always done, fully aware of the consequences. He faced toward Jerusalem as he prayed (perhaps influenced by Solomon's prayer, 1 Kings 8:44-45,48; 2 Chron. 6:34). His enemies immediately informed the king that Daniel had violated the decree and must suffer the consequences. Their reminder to the king that Daniel was one of the "exiles from Judah" (v. 13) may reveal that their hatred found its roots in racial prejudice.

Daniel's Sentencing and Deliverance (6:14-28)

The king was distressed and made every legal effort to deliver Daniel from his own foolish decree but without success. Sorrowfully, he ordered the sentence to be carried out after expressing a hope to Daniel that somehow Daniel's God might save him (v. 16). The mouth of the pit was sealed with the seals of the king and his lords to prevent an illegal rescue of Daniel. The king was unable to eat or sleep that night.

Early the next morning the king hastened to the lions' den and cried out in anguish for Daniel to respond if he were still alive. To the king's astonishment, he heard Daniel calmly reply that God had sent his angel to shut the lions' mouths because Daniel was innocent before God and the king (compare Heb. 11:33).

The king called for Daniel's release and then ordered all those who had plotted against Daniel, including their families, to be cast to the lions. The account of their fate ends on a grisly note that the lions began tearing them apart even before their bodies touched the bottom of the den.

The king then issued a decree to be proclaimed throughout the empire, ordering all his subjects to tremble and fear before Daniel's God, for he was the living, eternal God who had rescued Daniel from the lions. The decree need not be interpreted as an order for the Persian subjects to abandon their other gods and worship only the Lord, for nothing like this happened during the years of Persian domination of the ancient Near East. It only meant that the people were required to recognize that Daniel's God was truly a god. In the polytheistic world of Daniel, such a decree would have created no problem.

The chapter closes with a statement that Daniel continued to prosper "during the reign of Darius and the reign of Cyrus the Persian" (v. 28). The mention of Darius raises again the problem that was discussed with 5:31. A number of scholars have proposed that the problem here can be solved by translating verse 28 as "during the reign of Darius, that is, the reign of Cyrus the Persian," as the Hebrew word for *and* can be translated as "that is" (see, for example, "the spirit of Pul king of Assyria [that is, Tiglath-Pileser king of Assyria]," 1 Chron. 5:26, NIV; see also NEB). Thus, further support is given for the contention that Darius and Cyrus were one and the same.

The Visions of Daniel
7:1 to 12:13

A Vision of Four Animals and the Son of Man (7:1-28)

In chapters 1—6 the narratives of the Book of Daniel are recorded in story form and are for the most part related in the third person. In chapters 7—12 the presentation is different. In these chapters Daniel relates experiences that came to him as visions in dreams. Chronologically chapters 7 and 8 belong before chapter 5 because these visions occurred during the reign of Belshazzar (7:1; 8:1). It is obvious, therefore, that Daniel's visions were deliberately grouped together as we find them in chapters 7—12. Chapter 7 appropriately forms a link with the chapters that have preceded and the chapters that follow. It has been called one of the most important chapters in the Old Testament.

The Vision (7:1-14)

Daniel's first vision, which he carefully recorded, occurred during the first year of Belshazzar's reign (v. 1; see the introduction to 5:1-30 for a discussion of Belshazzar as king). The vision was of four ominous-appearing beasts that rose out of the sea. The fourth beast had ten horns, and, as Daniel watched, a little horn grew up that uprooted three of the first horns (vv. 7-8).

Then the scene shifted to a court that was sitting in judgment, presided over by an "ancient of days." As a result of the judgment, the fourth beast was slain, and the other beasts were stripped of their dominion (vv. 11-12). Then Daniel saw one who was "like a son of man," a heavenly being in human form and clearly a messianic figure. He was presented before the "Ancient of Days" (v. 13). Everlasting dominion was given to the "son of man."

The Interpretation of the Vision (7:15-28)

Daniel inquired concerning the meaning of what he had seen and was told that the four beasts represented four kings ("kingdoms" in v. 23). He was also told that ultimately the kingdom will be possessed by the "saints of the Most High" (vv. 17-18). These "saints" have been interpreted as Jews or, in a more general sense, as all those who are faithful to God.

Daniel inquired further about the fourth beast because it was so different from the others (v. 19). He was told that the beast represented a fourth kingdom, differing from all the others, that would conquer the whole earth. Parallels with the four kingdoms of Nebuchadnezzar's dream image of chapter 2 are apparent, and the two chapters should be interpreted together. They both describe the same four kingdoms and God's ultimate exaltation over all earthly kingdoms.

Daniel was told further that the ten horns of the beast represented ten kings and that the little horn represented another king who will arise after them (v. 24). This last king will speak boldly against the Most High, persecute the saints, and attempt to change the times and the law. He will be successful for three and a half "times" (usually understood as "years"), but then his dominion will be taken from him. The kingdom will be given to the "people of the saints of the Most High" (v. 27) and will endure forever.

Some interpreters explain the four kingdoms of Daniel's vision as Babylon, Medo-Persia, Greece, and Rome. They explain the ten horns as a revived Roman empire ruled by ten contemporary kings. The little horn coming from the fourth beast represents the Antichrist, who will persecute believers during the three and one-half years of the Great Tribulation (see Rev. 11:2; 13:5). He will rule over the revived Roman empire, but he will be overthrown by divine intervention, and the kingdom of God will be established forever.

Other interpreters say the four successive kingdoms are Babylon, Media, Persia, and Greece. There is disagreement among these interpreters as to the identity of the ten historical kings represented by the ten horns of the fourth kingdom. However, there is agreement that the "little horn" is Antiochus IV (Epiphanes), who attempted to suppress the Jewish laws and religious practices from 168-165 BC. He was a Seleucid ruler, a family that gained control of Syria and Palestine after the division of the Greek empire following the death of Alexander the Great. The Jewish people rose up in rebellion against him under the leadership of a family named Maccabee, and they were successful in regaining their independence in 165 BC.

Regardless of different interpretations, chapter 7 contains a message that all can agree on. The "Most High" is the sovereign God of heaven and earth. He will be victorious over all those who oppose him, and those who are identified with him will share in that triumph. The message of chapter 7 is timeless: God will be victorious over all evil, and the faithful will share in the kingdom he will establish.

A Vision of a Ram and a He-Goat (8:1-27)

The vision of chapter 8 is closely related to the vision of chapter 7 and in some respects is dependent on it for its interpretation. In chapter 8 the language changes back to Hebrew from the Aramaic used in 2:4*b* to 7:28.

The Vision (8:1-14)

In the third year of Belshazzar's reign (550/549 BC), Daniel was transported in a vision to the river Ulai, a manmade canal located near the Persian city of Susa (or Shushan, the ancient capital of Elam). Ezekiel and the apostle John experienced similar visionary transport to other places (Ezek. 8:3; Rev. 17:3). At the Ulai Daniel observed a two-horned ram standing near the river. One of its two horns was longer than the other. The ram's power was so great that he overcame all other animals that challenged him.

As Daniel continued to watch the ram, he noticed a he-goat with a large horn growing from between his eyes, like the legendary unicorn. The he-goat came charging from the west with great speed against the ram, knocked him down, and trampled on him. Even as he exulted in his victory, his large horn was broken off and replaced by four horns. Out of them came a little horn that grew until it reached toward heaven. It defiantly set itself up to be as great as the "Prince of the host" (v. 11; that is, God). It abolished the daily burnt offerings to the prince and desecrated his sanctuary. The little horn prospered in everything it did.

Then Daniel heard two holy ones conversing. One asked the other how long it would take for the vision to be fulfilled. The answer which Daniel heard was 2,300 evenings and mornings, after which the sanctuary would be restored. Two thousand three hundred "evenings and mornings" has been interpreted to mean 2,300 days and also to mean 1,150 days (an evening and a morning being equal to one day), or approximately three and one-half years.

The Interpretation of the Vision (8:15-27)

The angel Gabriel appeared to explain the vision to Daniel, which was for "the time of the end" (v. 17). This is the first time in the Bible that an angel is called by name. Strangely, at that moment Daniel fell asleep (or perhaps fainted) and had to be awakened by Gabriel before he continued to interpret the vision for Daniel.

The meaning of the vision is not left in doubt. Gabriel said that the animal with the two horns represented the kings of Media and Persia (v. 20). The fact that the horns were both on the same animal and that one was larger than the other has been used as support by scholars who believe that the second kingdom (see 2:39; 7:5) should be understood as the combined Medo-Persian empire, rather than successive empires of Media and Persia. They point out that there never really was a separate Median world empire that preceded the Persian empire. The taller horn, then, represented Persia that, under the leadership of Cyrus, defeated Astyages the king of Media in 550 BC and established the joint Medo-Persian empire.

Gabriel then explained that the he-goat represented the king of Greece (that is, the Greek empire), and the large horn between its eyes represented its first king (v. 21). That first king, of course, was Alexander the Great, who overthrew the Persian empire. Upon his sudden death at age thirty-two, however, there was no successor to keep the Greek empire intact that he had forged, so it was divided among his generals. This division into four kingdoms is symbolized in verse 22 by the four horns that rose in place of the single large horn. Their power would not be as great as that of the first kingdom.

Verses 23-24 introduce a "king of bold countenance," a man of great power who will cause fearful destruction and the death of many people. He will even rise up against the "Prince of princes" but will be supernaturally destroyed ("by no human hand, he shall be broken," v. 25).

There is general agreement that the little horn of chapter 8, this "king of bold countenance," is Antiochus IV (Epiphanes), even among those scholars who interpret the little horn of chapter 7 as the Antichrist. The little horn of 8:9,23 grew out of the four horns (the four Greek kingdoms), whereas the little horn of 7:8,24 uprooted three of the ten horns of the fourth beast.

Antiochus returned from a humiliating defeat at the hands of the Romans in Egypt in 168 BC and took out his frustration on the Jews in Jerusalem. He killed or enslaved many of them and by decree tried to abolish their religious practices. He abolished their laws regarding the sabbath, circumcision, and food restrictions on pain of death and erected an altar to Zeus over the altar of burnt offering in the Temple. The Jews rebelled, and led by a family named Maccabee, were successful in restoring worship in the Temple in 165 BC. The "king of fierce countenance" described in Daniel 8 could be none other than Antiochus IV (Epiphanes), described accurately in the chapter as scheming, treacherous, and defiant of God. Altogether, his persecution of the Jewish people lasted about three and one-half years.

Gabriel told Daniel to seal up the vision, for it concerned matters "many days hence" (v. 26). Daniel remained ill for some days at the conclusion of the vision before he was able to resume his royal duties. The vision left him shaken, and he confessed that he did not understand it (v. 27).

An Explanation of Jeremiah's Seventy Years (9:1-27)

The exact number of years that Daniel lived in exile cannot be determined, but he was still in Babylon over sixty years after being taken there by Nebuchadnezzar. During his years in exile he must have wondered frequently how long the Exile would last and whether he would ever return home. When Daniel read Jeremiah's statements that the years of punishment would total seventy, he turned to the Lord in a prayer of confession on behalf of his people.

Daniel's Prayer of Confession (9:1-19)

Verse 1 dates Daniel's prayer in the first year of the reign of Darius, called the son of Ahasuerus (see the comments on 5:31 for the problem of Darius' identity). The only Ahasuerus known from historical records was the son of Darius I (522-486). He succeeded his father and ruled Persia from 486 to 465 BC (see Esther 1:1; his Greek name was Xerxes).

The reader might have expected Daniel's prayer to be an appeal for understanding of Jeremiah's prophecy of seventy years of the Jewish Exile (Jer. 25:11-12; 29:10; see also 2 Chron. 36:21; Lev. 26:18,33-35). However, the prayer contains no mention of the seventy years. Rather, it is Daniel's confession on behalf of his people's sins and an appeal for forgiveness. Apparently Daniel knew that if they were ever to return home, they must repent and be forgiven.

Daniel is not the only one in the Scriptures who confessed the sins of his people and interceded for them. Other intercessors included Moses (Ex. 32:31-32), Samuel (1 Sam. 12:23), Solomon (1 Kings 8:34-50), Amos (Amos 7:2), Jeremiah (Jer. 7:16), Ezra (Ezra 9:6-15), and Nehemiah (Neh. 1:6-11).

Daniel's prayer is a model for the confession of sins. True confession includes a spirit of humility (v. 3), acknowledgment of the greatness and faithfulness of God (v. 4), a confession of the sins committed (vv. 5-11), and an appeal for forgiveness and restoration of favor (vv. 15-19).

Gabriel's Explanation of the Seventy Years (9:20-27)

While Daniel was praying, the angel Gabriel came and announced that he would explain the meaning of Jeremiah's "Seventy weeks of years" to Daniel. Gabriel's interpretation goes far beyond the literal seventy years that Jeremiah spoke about.

Gabriel explained that Jeremiah's seventy years represented "Seventy weeks of years" (literally "seventy sevens," that is, 490 years). That would be the period of time required for the completion of Jerusalem's punishment and "to bring in everlasting righteousness" (v. 24).

Then Gabriel described the phases of the "seventy weeks of years." The first, "seven weeks . . . sixty-two weeks," represented the time from the decree to rebuild Jerusalem to the coming of an

anointed prince (v. 25). At the end of that time an anointed one will
be cut off, and the city and the Temple will be destroyed by the
people of another prince (v. 26).

During the remaining one week (that is, seven years) this evil
prince will make a covenant with many people, but during the
second half of the week he will abolish the Temple worship and
sacrifices. Then one will come "on the wing of abominations" who
makes desolate, but judgment will overtake him (v. 27).

Gabriel's explanation of Jeremiah's seventy years has become one
of the major controversial passages in the Old Testament. As was
true of the interpretation of chapter 7, one interpretation is given by
those who believe the passage speaks of things yet to come and
another is given by those who believe that the passage describes
things that have already happened. (For a good summary of the
many interpretations see the Daniel commentary in the *International Critical Commentary* series by J. A. Montgomery, pp.
390-401; and the *Tyndale Old Testament Commentaries* series by
Joyce Baldwin, pp. 172-78.)

Some interpreters say that the first sixty-nine weeks were completed with the crucifixion ("an anointed one shall be cut off," v. 26).
This event has been followed by the "church age" of an indetermi-
nate time. The final, or seventieth week (a period of seven years), is
yet future and will mark the time of the great tribulation. It will
begin with the rapture of Christians. The Antichrist, a world ruler,
will reveal himself halfway through the seven-year period and will
institute a terrible era of suffering and tribulation for the remaining
three and one-half years. The end of that seventieth week will be
marked by the second coming of Christ and the battle of Armageddon that will usher in the millennium.

A second interpretation says the seventy weeks were completed
with the destruction of Jerusalem by the Romans in AD 70.

Other interpreters explain the first seven weeks as the period
from the destruction of Jerusalem to Cyrus's decree that allowed the
Jews to return home (587-538 BC). The next sixty-two weeks include
the years from 538 to 171 BC. The seventieth week took place
between 171 and 165 BC, coinciding with the rule of Antiochus IV
(Epiphanes, "the desolator") over the Jews. The last three and one-
half years of that period were marked by his intensive persecution of
the Jews (see comments on 7:23-25).

Whether the emphasis of the interpretation of chapter 9 is placed on a yet future event or an event already historically completed, all can agree that the chapter teaches that God is triumphant over all evil.

A Vision About Things to Come (10:1 to 12:13)

The final vision contained in chapters 10—12 is the longest and most detailed oracle in the Book of Daniel. It occurred in the third year of Cyrus's rule (that is, 537 BC), about the time that the first group of exiles returned to Jerusalem. The vision gave further assurance to Daniel of the ultimate triumph of God's people over all the evil that they must endure. It describes approximately the same period of history as chapter 8.

Preparations for the Vision (10:1 to 11:1)

The vision was preceded by a time of mourning and fasting by Daniel that lasted three weeks (vv. 2-3). On the twenty-fourth day of the first month (the most specific date given for one of Daniel's messages), he was standing with some other men beside the Tigris River (called here "the great river," a designation ordinarily reserved for the Euphrates). No reason is given for his being at that particular place. Suddenly he saw a man of shining appearance and dressed in linen. The visitor has been identified by commentators as God himself (compare Ezek. 1:26-28), Gabriel, Michael, or an unnamed angel superior to all the other angels. Early Christian commentators said he was Christ (compare Rev. 1:12-16).

The other men with Daniel were unable to see the vision; but they must have known that something unusual was taking place, for they ran away in fear (v. 7). All Daniel's strength drained from his body, and he turned deathly pale. Upon hearing the voice of the supernatural visitor, he fell into a deep sleep (or perhaps fainted).

The divine visitor told Daniel to stand up (compare the Lord's words to Ezekiel, Ezek. 2:1) and to have no fear. He informed Daniel that the "prince of the kingdom of Persia" had withstood him twenty-one days, but Michael came to his assistance. This "prince" has usually been identified by commentators as a guardian angel of Persia, just as Michael was the guardian angel of Israel. The one speaking with Daniel said he left Michael with the "prince of the kingdom of Persia" (RSV, but the Hebrew says "I remained there with the kings of Persia") in order to come and tell Daniel what was going to happen to the Jewish people "in the latter days" (v. 14).

The words left Daniel speechless (v. 15). One "like the sons of men," probably the same divine being who had been speaking to Daniel, touched Daniel's lips, and he was able to speak again. Daniel complained that the vision had left him without any strength (v. 17). Still clothed in human form, the visitor touched Daniel, and his assurances strengthened Daniel.

He then informed Daniel that he must return to fight against the prince of Persia, and after him, the prince of Greece. He was anticipating the oppression of the Lord's people by both these foreign powers. He added that only Michael was helping him in the fight against these enemies. Michael is mentioned only three times in the Old Testament, all in Daniel (10:13,21; 12:1), and twice in the New Testament (Jude 9; Rev. 12:7).

Verse 1 of chapter 11 more appropriately belongs with the end of chapter 10 than with the beginning of the following chapter. It tells the reader that the one speaking to Daniel had helped Michael during the first year of the reign of Darius (see 5:31 for discussion of the identity of Darius).

A Revelation of Events in History (11:2 to 12:4)

Chapter 11 deals with only two of the world empires previously introduced by Daniel, the Persian and the Greek empires. In this respect it is parallel to chapter 8. Chapter 11 gives a detailed account of the Ptolemaic rulers of Egypt and the Seleucid rulers of Syria but calls them "the king of the south" and "the king of the north." There is no agreement whether "at the time of the end" (v. 40) refers to the end of the rule of a particular historical tyrant, Antiochus IV (Epiphanes), or whether it anticipates a yet future oppressor.

The kings of Persia and the king of Greece (11:2-4).—Daniel was told there would be three more kings in Persia, followed by a fourth king who would go to war with Greece. If Cyrus (550-530 BC) is counted as the first, then the other three Persian kings are Cambyses (530-522), Darius I (522-486), and Xerxes I (486-465), who attacked Greece in 480 and took Athens. Subsequent defeats, however, finally forced him to withdraw from Europe altogether.

If Cyrus is not counted as the first king, then in order to have four kings, Gaumata (Pseudo-Smerdis), a usurper who ruled for about seven months in 522 before being overthrown by Darius, would have to be included.

The mighty ruler described in verses 3-4 who will arise but whose kingdom will be divided among those who are not his descendants could be none other than Alexander the Great (336-323), whose empire was divided after his death.

Conflicts between the southern and northern kings (11:5-20).— After Alexander's death his empire was divided among four of his generals. One of them, Seleucus, received the area that included Syria and Palestine. His dynasty is represented by "the king of the north" in these verses. Another general, Ptolemy, became ruler of Egypt. His dynasty is the one referred to as "the king of the south" in these verses.

Verse 5 describes a prince of the king of the south who will become stronger than the king himself. Historically, this "prince" was Seleucus, an officer in Alexander's army who was appointed satrap (governor) of Babylon in 321 BC. Challenged in 316 BC by Antigonus, another of Alexander's generals, he was forced to seek refuge with Ptolemy in Egypt. Ptolemy made him a general, and with Egyptian help Seleucus was able to regain his satrapy in 312 BC. At the battle of Ipsus in 301 BC Seleucus defeated Antigonus and eventually gained control of an empire that extended from Phrygia in the west almost to the Indus River in the east. With these victories Seleucus controlled an empire much larger than Ptolemy's.

Verse 6 describes an alliance by marriage of the daughter of the king of the south to the king of the north but adds that the offspring of that marriage will not maintain the throne. Historically, this is a description of the marriage between Berenice, daughter of Ptolemy II, to Antiochus II about 249 BC. The marriage was arranged for the purpose of terminating the wars between Egypt and Syria. The conditions of the agreement were that Antiochus would divorce his wife Laodice and that his sons would renounce their claim on Syria's throne. In this way Ptolemy hoped to gain Syria as an Egyptian province. However, he died shortly after the marriage. Then Antiochus divorced Berenice ("she shall not retain the strength of her arm") and took back his first wife, Laodice, who subsequently had him poisoned. As a result of his death, Laodice's son Seleucus became king. One of his first acts was to murder Berenice and her infant child in order to secure the throne for himself.

Verses 7-9 describe an invasion from the south that will be

successful. Much spoil will be taken from the north. Then later the king of the north will invade the south but will return to his own land. Historically, these verses describe a brother of Berenice, Ptolemy III, who in revenge for his sister's murder invaded Syria, then ruled by Seleucus II. He overran a large part of Seleucus's kingdom and carried away a vast amount of booty. However, trouble in Egypt forced him to return home. Two years later Seleucus II invaded Egypt only to be defeated decisively by Ptolemy III and forced to flee back to Syria.

Verses 10-19 describe a succession of battles between the kings of the north and of the south. Verses 10-12 describe a victory won by the king of the south over the king of the north. Historically the verses describe Antiochus III, who made war against Egypt, ruled by Ptolemy IV. After a series of battles Antiochus was defeated decisively by Ptolemy.

Verses 13-17a indicate that the king of the north will raise another army and have a great victory over the king of the south. Historically, these verses parallel the events that took place after the death of Ptolemy IV and the succession of his four-year old son, Ptolemy V, in 203 BC. Antiochus III took advantage of the situation and made an alliance with Philip V of Macedon by which both joined in an attack on Egypt. The outcome was a decisive defeat for the Egyptian army led by its general, Scopas.

Verse 17b describes a marriage that will be made to seal the peace. Antiochus III decided that it was to his advantage to make peace with Ptolemy V because of political ambitions in other directions. He gave his daughter Cleopatra to Ptolemy in marriage in the year 194 BC in order to gain Ptolemy's favor and also to promote his interests in Egypt.

Verses 18-19 say that the king of the north will then return home but will be overthrown. In 192 Antiochus III invaded Greece but was defeated by the Romans, who determined to drive him completely out of Asia Minor. At the battle of Magnesia in 190, Antiochus suffered a humiliating defeat. He had to submit to the Roman terms for peace and had to abandon all claims on Asia Minor. The Seleucid empire's power reached a low point as a result of Antiochus's defeat at the hands of the Romans.

Verse 20 describes a successor to the northern ruler who will be "broken" in a short time. The northern ruler, Antiochus III, had two sons. The first, Seleucus IV, succeeded his father but was murdered in a conspiracy after an uneventful twelve-year rule.

The rise of a contemptible ruler (11:21-45).—These verses describe a successor to the northern ruler who had been "broken" (see v. 20). He is described as a contemptible, deceitful, and powerful ruler. He will have a great victory over the king of the south (vv. 25-28). Historically, this "contemptible" ruler was Antiochus IV (Epiphanes, 175-164 BC). He was not actually the legitimate successor to the throne. Seleucus IV had a son, Demetrius, who was the rightful heir, but he was being held hostage in Rome; so Seleucus's younger brother, Antiochus, claimed the throne for himself in 175 BC.

Antiochus invaded Egypt in 170 and captured Ptolemy Philometor. He pretended to support the claims of Philometor to the throne of Egypt as he, meanwhile, was gaining control over all of Egypt. He was called back to Syria for a short time to quell a revolt instigated by the deposed high priest, Jason, who had heard a rumor that Antiochus had been killed in Egypt.

Verses 29-39 describe a second campaign into the south that will not be so successful as the first. Forced to turn back and in a rage, he will take action against the "holy covenant" (v. 30). The continual burnt offering will be abolished and the "abomination that makes desolate" will be set up (v. 31). Some of the people will support him, but those who know God will stand against him. This king will become so proud that he will exalt himself above every god and will worship gods his fathers did not know (vv. 36-39).

Verses 29-39 describe the following historical events. While Antiochus was in Syria, the Egyptians made Ptolemy Physcon, a brother of Philometor, their king. Antiochus returned in 169 BC on the pretext that he was supporting Philometor's claim to the Egyptian throne. Other matters called him back to Syria for a short time, but then he returned to Egypt in 168 BC to complete his conquest of that land after learning that the two Ptolemys had reconciled their differences and were reigning jointly.

Near Alexandria he was met by representatives of Rome who gave him an ultimatum to leave Egypt. Humiliated and frustrated by his defeat at the hands of the Romans, he returned to Syria in a rage and vented his anger on the Jews ("take action against the holy covenant," v. 30). He determined to obliterate every trace of the Jewish religion by abolishing their sacrifices and laws. The sacred

Temple was transformed into a shrine to Zeus, a Greek god, and unclean animals were offered on the altar. This blasphemous act provoked the Jews to open rebellion. Led by a man named Mattathias Maccabee and his sons, the Jews regained their independence in 165 and reestablished their worship practices in the Temple.

Verses 40-45 describe the fate of the "king of the north." "At the time of the end" the king of the south will attack him, but the king of the north will have a great victory, and many lands will come under his domination. But then the king of the north will receive disturbing news from the east and the north that will incite him to dispatch his troops to destroy this new threat. The text does not give the outcome of the struggle but suggests his defeat by the words, "He shall come to his end, with none to help him" (v. 45).

There is agreement among scholars that verses 21-35 describe accurately the reign of Antiochus IV. However, they do not agree concerning the interpretation of verses 36-45. Some say all these verses describe the reign of Antiochus IV and point out that the closing verse describes his death at Tabae in Persia while on an expedition in the east. Others say that verses 36-45 describe the activities of the Antichrist in the time of the great tribulation.

A coming resurrection (12:1-4).—Daniel described a "time of trouble" from which those would be delivered whose names were "written in the book" (v. 1). The Old Testament frequently speaks of a record that God keeps of those who are his elect people (Ex. 32:32; Ps. 69:28; Mal. 3:16; Luke 10:20; Rev. 20:12). Daniel also foresaw a universal resurrection of the dead. This resurrection will usher some into eternal life, but for others it will mean everlasting contempt (v. 2).

The clearest statement about resurrection in the Old Testament is found in verse 2 (see also Isa. 26:19). It is difficult to know how the Hebrews perceived life after death, as the Old Testament does not give a clear description of their beliefs about afterlife. Their concept of a living God who loved them and wanted to deliver them enabled them to grasp a conviction that his life would be imparted to them also.

Daniel was then told to seal up the revelation which had been given to him until the time of the end when the messages would be fulfilled (v. 4).

Final Words to Daniel (12:5-13)

As Daniel's vision was drawing to an end, a question was asked of the man clothed in linen (see 10:5 for a discussion of his identity): How long would it be until the fulfillment of the things Daniel had seen in his vision? The only answer given was that it would be "for a time, two times, and half a time" (v. 7; see explanation of this phrase in 7:25). The man dressed in linen refused to answer any more of Daniel's questions and said, "The words are shut up and sealed until the time of the end" (v. 9).

He added that there would be 1,290 days between the time the continual burnt offering was abolished and the setting up of the abomination that makes desolate. This period of time is interpreted by some as a reference to the Jewish persecutions under Antiochus IV and by others as events during the most severe phase of the great tribulation.

Then Daniel's visitor pronounced a blessing on those who wait and come to the 1,335 days (1,290 plus 45 days). Some interpret this period of time as the three and one-half years of Jewish persecution by Antiochus IV plus an additional forty-five days needed to establish the new Jewish state achieved by the successful revolt against Antiochus.

Others believe the 1335 days include the entire three and one-half years of the great tribulation plus the first days of the millennium. It is difficult to find an interpretation of the numbers 1,150 (8:14: "two thousand and three hundred evenings and mornings"), 1,290 (12:11), and 1,335 (12:12) that can be agreed upon by Bible scholars.

Then the man dressed in linen dismissed Daniel with the assurance that he would stand in his allotted place at the end of the days (v. 13). These words are apparently a reference to Daniel's ultimate resurrection. Thus, the book ends on a positive note of anticipation of the glorious future that awaits God's faithful people at the end of the age.